THANK YOU for writing ~~....~~ en
trying to convey to people i~~.. y....~~ ...~~.. ...~~...~~...~~...~~.de
for this. A few sections made me quite literally laugh out loud. What
amazing memories, and you remembered so many details! I never realized how unheard of things like the human knot or compliment circles
were. How incredible! The whole section about physical contact, something that 11-year-olds can find totally uncomfortable, was absolutely
building confidence and trust. It was FUN! We didn't realize you were
basically crushing barriers and building our confidence without us even
knowing. This manuscript bounces from "teacher training" to dissecting
the text to reminiscing to paying tribute. It's everything. There's so very
little that's left out. I'm not trying to be hyperbolic in any of this. I'm just
so grateful. It tells our story beautifully.

— Kendal Peiguss, actor

I'VE SEEN the transformative power of *Shakespeare's Spell* first-hand.
In Mr. DeWeese's classroom, my painfully shy and fearful 10-year-old
daughter experienced a safe environment in which she could take the
kind of risks that lead to self-knowledge and self-trust. Almost 10 years
after her immersion in the world of Shakespeare, I see a confident and
comfortable young woman who was deeply and positively affected by
the community- and trust-building exercises, the use of "masks," and the
many other techniques articulated so well in Mr. DeWeese's book.

My hope is that this book will reach the hearts and minds of many
teachers, who will steward Shakespeare and the ideas contained in
Shakespeare's Spell into the lives of some very fortunate kids.

— Tim Beckstrom, parent

AS EACH class worked together during the school year, students
memorized lines, struggled to "get inside" their characters, and confront-
ed the challenges of integrating it all into public performances. Often the
kids saw that what was happening in the plays mirrored their own struggles in real life. In quotes from the kids, we learn how they felt during
this process, and how the experience transformed them as individuals.

Reading the book is a delightful intellectual and emotional experience.

The author clearly knows and deeply respects the Shakespearean plays. And we start to see the plays as thrilling dramatic experiences, rather than just words on a printed page. We feel the kids' highs and the lows as they take on giant challenges. And, with the larger community, we celebrate the successful performances of both kids and author.

— Libby Palmer, teacher

THIS IS a book that should be required reading for any teacher who works with teens or pre-teens. First, it is not just a "how to" book. It gets you to a place where you can see not only "how to," but more importantly, "why to." Making drama integral to any subject matter results in a number of rather magical connections, within individual kids as well as within a class. It can transform a standard curriculum into a life-changing experience.

I taught alongside Bob for many years, and watched much of this firsthand. The intensity, dedication, and results apparent in this project are beyond anything normally seen in school. Doing drama productions like these is a huge commitment of time and energy in an already over-taxed curriculum, but if there was ever a way to get more value out of time spent, this is it. It is not an "extra." It is the window to the core of it all.

In the book, Bob shares many of the reflections written by his students that give some sense of this. Their comments are from the heart, and give a huge insight into the experience. In a culture where kids, especially teens, seem to have so little opportunity for meaningful connections, doing this type of drama is a golden invitation for truly internalizing curriculum, enhancing personal growth, and gaining a strong sense of community and belonging. Though the process may be painful at times, I've seen many shy and unsure young folks emerge from these productions as confident and creative people, ready to move on in their lives with a strong new sense of identity and direction. What more valuable experience can a teacher hope to offer?

— Sue Dazey, teacher

*A*ll the power this charm doth owe…

– SHAKESPEARE, A MIDSUMMER NIGHT'S DREAM

For Tracy –

"But we are spirits
of another sort…"
(Oberon)

Thanks for being part of the
magic!

with love!

Bob DenLoese

All the Power This Charm Doth Owe:

TEACHING UNDER
SHAKESPEARE'S SPELL

by

ROBERT DeWEESE

PUBLISHED BY
TURTLE PRESS
Port Townsend, WA

ALL THE POWER THIS CHARM DOTH OWE:
TEACHING UNDER SHAKESPEARE'S SPELL

by Robert DeWeese

Copyright 2015, Robert DeWeese

Published by
Turtle Press
P.O. Box 158, Port Townsend, WA 98368
(360) 385-3626

Book design by
Ruth Marcus, Sequim, WA

ISBN 978-0-965-1963-4-5

Typeset in Minion

A Note to the Reader

Although my name is on the title page of this book as author, it is actually a collaborative effort, even an anthology of sorts.

I did theater with my students for 15 years. In that period, we produced and performed some 40 plays. Every student in my classroom had a speaking role in each play, and for every production I used multiple casts, in order to give students a better chance at getting good parts. Each cast went through dress rehearsals and gave at least two (sometimes four or five) performances—daytime shows for other classes, and evening performances for a wider audience. This process took a lot of time and effort, and we did a lot of after-school rehearsing.

Starting in 2000, I also directed an after-school theater class, attended by older students who had graduated out of our program. This group, which started as "Shakespeare After School" and after a few years became "Changeling," usually included enough actors to make up two casts, and performed three to five shows, depending on the size of the group.

After every production, I asked the students to write about their thoughts, feelings, and experiences. Afterwards, I collated their responses, gave them each a copy, and kept a copy for my files.

In the following pages, you will read their words and hear their voices—these are set off from the main text and italicized. The great majority of these passages are directly from my surveys. The longer responses are reflection essays, written later on in their academic careers, and selections from personal letters and emails to me.

The paragraph in the introduction, about wearing a mask, is from a note I found on my bulletin board one morning as I was preparing for class. The author of that note was one of many students whose life was changed by what we did together. I hope someday she will read this anthology, and see how profoundly my life was changed as well.

For my family, and for the actors.

Now upon thy eye I throw
All the power this charm doth owe.

Contents

Introduction: I Am to Discourse Wonders

A Midsummer Night's Dream, last scene: Puck's *Please don't be offended— it was just a silly dream—we'll make it up to you* epilogue. A sixth-grader appears out of the upstage darkness and walks down into the spotlight. A year past her family's messy break-up, and still caught in the bitter middle of it, she has taken obsessive refuge in the other world of Shakespeare. For this role, she is wearing green tights and green leggings, and her artist mother has hand-painted her face, arms, and neck in beautiful braidings of English ivy.

She is fascinated by the epilogue. Who is saying it? Puck—and if so, which version, Robin Goodfellow the benevolent spirit, Hobgoblin Puck the bad boy, or both? Or is it being said by the actor playing Puck, as a way of leading the audience back into the "real world"? Or is it both at once.

After weeks of passionate fixation upon the role—and especially this scene—she decides that the third choice is the only possible solution.

Stepping into the spot, while beginning to speak the speech—and she speaks strongly, her Puck is obviously not really sorry at all, and wants only to further mystify the audience—she dips two fingers into a small bowl of water we now see she is holding; and as she speaks, she begins to remove her make-up.

> *And as I am an honest Puck,*
> *if we have unearned luck*
> *now to 'scape the serpent's tongue,*

we will make amends ere long,
else the Puck a liar call.
So, good night unto you all.
Give me your hands, if we be friends,
and Robin will restore amends.

The spot fades out, and she is left alone, transcendence slowly ebbing away. A girl on the edge of adolescence, trying to come to terms with her life, learning to move in and out of a different world. Like an actor playing Puck.

When I look back, I feel like it was just the best dream I've
ever had. When I look at the pictures of myself onstage, I
laugh, and get that magical little tingle in my fingers. And
I remember what fun it was, how I wanted to do this the rest
of my life. How I'd be just standing on the stage, more than
anything else, knowing who I really was.

The 12' x 16' stage in our classroom was only sixteen inches high. But for so many young people with whom I did theater, taking that single small step up was extremely transformative. Instead of a form of pretending that isolated, they learned a kind that connected them—to each other, to the bottomless deeps of Shakespeare's texts, to the infinite possibilities of dramatic art, and—especially—to the unguessed-at riches of their own personalities. Coming into our class, trying to hide, many were lost. Learning to trust, and pretending to be someone else, almost all of them found their way.

I was Lysander, a fairy, Hermia, Puck, Biron, and Beatrice.
I'm nineteen now and today I came back to this room to
remember how it felt. I haven't been onstage since I left but
the memories don't fade. I still think about the two years I
spent here and how they've shaped me. Thank you for
teaching me how to wear a mask, and how to take it off.

The impulse to hide, to wear a mask, is a central theme of adolescence. One of the most troubled students I ever taught, one of the few who proved to be physically dangerous to his sibling and his fellow students, declared early on his great fondness for hermit crabs, and kept several as "pets." Their armored invulnerability personified his fear and anger. Sometimes, the power of one adolescent's urge to hide and/or armor himself can change the dynamics of a whole classroom. And in many cases, efforts to counsel a young person back from isolation prove futile.

What might happen if, instead of trying to expose their vulnerabilities, students were *offered* masks? What if, instead of insisting that they "build on their strengths" or "be true to themselves," they were given emotional amnesty, and the opportunity to try out a whole range of different roles? What might happen if, instead of locking them down in hand-held electronic prisons, we showed them a gallery of interesting people to pretend to be?

> *Performing the play meant showing a side of yourself that you don't normally see. And by seeing that side of yourself, you can help yourself, you can express yourself in that new way.*

> *Being able to become a different person and forget all the problems going on offstage has meant so much to me this year. Feeling what another human would feel, even that person's problems, was so brilliant. Shakespeare has made me look at life from a different perspective.*

> *Becoming another person onstage and forgetting everything else is amazing. I feel a lot happier. Doing drama gives me a light, happy feeling—very bouncy. I can be a different person, with different feelings. I feel unique.*

> *Each time I played Titania I got better. It changed me a lot. Sometimes I'm home doing whatever and I close my eyes and I feel like Titania again and being mad. Drama has made me*

open up as a person, and I don't feel nervous or scared any more. And I don't feel shy any more, I feel like a new me. I made new friends. I feel more open to the world.

The play taught me that anything can come true ("dreams, wishes, tears, poor fancy's followers"). It also brought out a new side of me this year that I've never really seen before. It taught me how to talk and act in a different way.

When I'm onstage, the shy girl deep down inside of me vanishes. I can just let myself act. I like knowing that I'm a lot like Puck, but also a lot like Helena.

I remember how I felt onstage when I was my character. I felt free, and I didn't have to be myself, which I liked most of all.

I can let myself loose on the stage. It has given me more of a personality.

An actor can leave his own self behind and be a totally different person. And we carry that person with us everywhere.

If I didn't have acting, I wouldn't know myself. Drama has taught me things I didn't know about me, and has helped me be a better person.

It makes me feel more happy and alive—I feel fuller as a person when I perform or finish performing a play. I feel like I've been someone else, seen a life through someone else's eyes, and that alone has changed me very much.

Drama is a passion. It's a place where you change and feel things. It's not a place where you hide, it's a place to figure out what you're hiding from.

For 15 years, two or three or sometimes even four times a year, during and after school, I did real theater with students between the ages of 10 and 18. After several months of sporadic rehearsals, after an intense two weeks of dress rehearsals and performances, they wrote about their experiences. What do you remember? What were your favorite lines and scenes—and why? What did the play mean to you personally? How did you decide how to play your character? What made the play work? In what ways, if any, has doing drama made a difference for you? What did you learn about yourself? About your fellow actors? Who/what helped you the most, and how? Compare this play to the previous one. And so on.

Almost invariably, students were eager to respond, even the reluctant writers. The long process of preparing the play, building trust among cast members, and pushing ourselves to get everything right was very intense. For one thing, most of the plays we did had been done in previous years by older students, and there were standards to uphold—or try to surpass. Also, the high quality of the material (80% Shakespeare, plus several productions of *Our Town* and similarly serious plays) challenged them to bring a like-minded seriousness to their practice. A successful production was a cause for strong feelings of relief and accomplishment, and responding to the surveys was a way to process it all.

In their words and mine, this is our story. How we learned, together, to make ourselves into a theater troupe. How we created the bonds of trust that made everything possible. How we made Shakespeare's words come alive. How we sustained each other with processing circles and crazy games. How we learned to believe in each other and ourselves, and looking back, what it meant to us in the end. How we found out who we really are.

> *It's like those little cars in the circus, you know? This tiny red*
> *car comes out, hardly big enough for a midget, and it putters*
> *around, and suddenly its doors open and out come a thousand*
> *clowns, whooping and hollering and raising hell.*
>   – Murray Burns, in *A Thousand Clowns*

> *Masters, I am to discourse wonders.*
>   – *A Midsummer Night's Dream*

photo by Isabel Gates

One side of Puck. [*A Midsummer Night's Dream*]

A Spirit of No Common Rate

Early in 1999, midway through the school year, I was at the low point of my teaching career. I was teaching fifth- and sixth-graders in a remarkable public school alternative program, and my students were bright, creative, and eccentric—all to my liking. But something wasn't clicking. I saw individual successes—kids doing great independent projects, for example—but somehow I could never get the whole group moving together toward a common goal.

Having come to teaching after years of environmental and political activism, I had high expectations. I expected to be able to nurture and lead my class in such a way that they became an engaged, involved cadre of teammates, working shoulder to shoulder to solve important problems.

But it hadn't happened. Although I couldn't justifiably complain that the kids weren't learning things they needed to learn, collaborative projects were difficult for them. The classroom dynamic was controlled by friendship groups—not quite cliques, but always moving in that direction. Kids new to the program, or perceived as too eccentric, tended to be left out. And although as a group we shared many of the same values and beliefs, inclusiveness didn't seem to be nearly as important to the kids as it was to me. As a result, in the middle of my fifth year as a teacher, I was mostly having to drag myself to school.

It wasn't as if I didn't have an idea what the answer might be. One of the best things about my teacher certification program six years earlier had been getting to know an incredible group of kindred spirits, one of whom was Ginger Montague. Ginger was a Seattle-area actress who had decided, in her late thirties, that she wanted to be a teacher. More specifically, she wanted to teach using drama as the central focus of her classroom. In class, she never missed an opportunity to expound, patiently but forcefully, on the magic of doing drama with kids.

Ginger and I hit it off from the first. Like me, she was an older student, trying out something new. Like me, she was an old lefty, an extrovert, and someone who thought that life in a classroom had to involve as much fun as possible. Every time we did one of the practice-teaching activities together, she would show all of us in the group how role-playing, drama games, and theater itself would make the activity more effective and more exciting.

I kept telling her that I had no training and no aptitude—that it was easy for her to talk, but the rest of us were just too shy. She would have none of it. She could tell that I was impressed with the possibilities, and she finally called me out. "You're gonna do it, and you know it," she said to me one day. "It's just a matter of how much time you're gonna waste before you decide not to be a chicken."

So I knew the answer to my dilemma. Still, was I desperate enough to try something with which I'd had no experience—in or out of the classroom? I knew, from listening to Ginger and from recognizing my own tendency to go all-in on projects, that this was not something one could do just a little of. If I did decide to do a play, it meant a huge time commitment, lots of parent support and involvement, and a major re-working of my curriculum.

And if I did it, what plays would I do? I had lost track of Ginger by then, and anyway, we had never reached the point of discussing which plays were best for which ages. Most of the classroom plays I had seen were either adapted fairy tales or morality plays, pushing a lesson about history or good behavior…not really the kind of thing I wanted. I knew in my heart that the only thing that would suit my purposes was something serious; it could be seriously funny, but it had to be something challenging and important enough to convince the kids (and me) that it was worth a huge commitment.

Before I started teaching, I spent 20 years in the second-hand book business, learning the out-of-print market and, with my family, running a small bookstore. One of the books I always searched for, because it was a perennial listing in the "Books Wanted" ads, was *Shake Hands with Shakespeare,* by Albert Cullum. After years of wondering whether this book actually existed, I had finally come across a battered paperback copy at a book sale. Too tattered to sell, the book joined my personal library of almost-rare curiosities.

Albert Cullum was semi-famous in the educational underground. His 1971 classic, *The Geranium on the Window Sill Just Died But Teacher You Went Right On,* was a beautiful and poetic attack on mindless, smiley-face teaching. Along with the more formal works of Jonathan Kozol, Herbert Kohl, John Holt, and A.S. Neill, Cullum's book was another protest against the dehumanizing practices of traditional American education. I treasured my copy, and shared it with my colleagues. I didn't know much about Albert Cullum, but I knew the most important thing: he was on the side of the kids.

The message of *Shake Hands with Shakespeare* was exactly what I needed to hear: here are some abridged scripts, using as much of the original language as possible; don't worry about costumes and props, use whatever; and—get going, you and the kids will love it. In the educational atmosphere of 1999, one already beginning to be dominated by technology and standardized testing, imagine how liberating it was to read this, written in the mid-60s:

> *Children should be performing plays, dances, and music, and in the doing, share their experiences with other students in their school.…Right within each elementary classroom is the nucleus of a Shakespearean repertory company—perhaps the most honest, the most direct, the most energetic performers a teacher can find.*

Cullum went directly to the heart of what is unique about doing Shakespeare—and at the same time, alleviated any worries a prospective director might have about expecting too much.

> *Shakespeare has the genius to encourage children to expose the hero within each young heart NOW. He brings to youngsters a reality and an exhilaration that everyday lesson plans do not.*

> *Don't worry if students do not comprehend all the subtleties and psychological implications of the plays. They will grasp the dominant ideas and understand the motivations at their own intelligence levels, and they will astound you with their perceptiveness in their discussions of the plays.*

The more I read, the more possibilities I began to see in trying out these new ideas. Of course I was desperate, and of course I badly wanted to believe that this was something I could learn to do. Then came the clincher—the answer to my despair about classroom dynamics.

> *My students have been presenting Shakespeare's plays and scenes in classrooms and for assemblies for many years. I have discovered that from the success of a play, <u>rapport develops in the classroom that creates mutual understanding and an eagerness to cooperate and learn together.</u>* [my emphasis] *After a final curtain with a classroom party, your class will have a unity that will astonish you.*

All kinds of curriculum ideas pop up in the life of a teacher. Every one of them promises to make your students smarter, your classroom easier to manage, and your own personal goals more easily achievable. For me, Albert Cullum's was the only vision that lived up to its promises.

Why Shakespeare? What is it about his words that make them *"metal more attractive"* than almost anything else in the English language? For Albert Cullum, the power was in the stories and the characters: *"...there is a passion for living in his words, and his thoughts are meaningful and tingling with implications. Children are touched by the greatness of Shakespeare, and they respond to and understand his characters and situations."* Quite true—but mightn't this be said about other writers?

There are countless explanations for Shakespeare's uniqueness and universal appeal, but how many apply to his fascination for young actors? His creative deviations from his sources—in sharpness of character portrayal and intensity of dramatic tension—were brilliant, but lost on my students. Likewise his enriching of the English language: they were impressed to hear of it, but that's not what makes him magical.

I believe that three factors sum up his ability to reach 400 years into the future and change young peoples' lives. One has to do with the content of the plays. Although it is true that very little in Shakespeare is black and white, there is a constant thread of compassion in the hearts of the characters who confront moral dilemmas.

> *Always in the Shakespearian world, harsh as the fate of man*
> *may be, there is someone like Kent, or Emilia, or Beatrice, or*
> *Paulina, who, disregarding personal danger and taking the*
> *rights of the case on faith, bursts out in angry indignation in the*
> *defense of the afflicted one.*
>   – Alfred Harbage, *As They Liked It*

Students recognize the strength of this recurring "kindness and graciousness," as Harbage calls it elsewhere, and respond to it instinctively. The moments within the plays we did where one character reaches out to another in emotional support were invariably among their favorites: Hippolyta's sympathy for Thisby, Beatrice's defense of Hero in the chapel, and Duke Senior's kindness to Adam and Orlando in *As You Like It* are only a few examples.

The second factor turns on a recent neurological discovery. Several years ago, Philip Davis at the University of Liverpool showed that Shakespeare's characteristic grammatical and syntactic creativity—using verbs as nouns, or adjectives as verbs, for instance—actually stimulates the brain to higher stages of connectivity:

> *By throwing odd words into seemingly normal sentences,*
> *Shakespeare surprises the brain and catches it off guard*
> *in a manner that produces a sudden burst of activity….*
> *the brain becomes positively excited. Experts believe this*
> *heightened brain activity may be one of the reasons why*
> *Shakespeare's plays have such a dramatic impact on their*
> *readers.*

In reading Shakespeare's scripts, middle-school kids seemed to have an advantage over older students: they were generally more open-minded about problematic language, and didn't continually insist on literal translations. What they called "the magic" had several sources. The challenge of something difficult, and the status of grappling with it, were undoubtedly important. But the singular ability of his texts to create an exciting, higher-order, puzzle-solving mental state was very real—even before I knew the explanation for it.

What really made Shakespeare a hit—the third and most significant factor—was acting it out. Dozens of students, over the years, said some version of this to me, or to one another: *"I didn't understand it when I read it, but when we blocked it out—I got it."* So many students, especially in alternative programs, are primarily kinesthetic learners. Grounding this strange and thrilling language in the movements of their bodies, practicing the coordination of lines and movements over and over, was by far the most effective means of making it real for them.

At first glance, some students—and especially the first class I gave it to—were intimidated. Shakespeare? Us? For many, it was like being asked to learn a foreign language. I was careful to offer definitions of unfamiliar words in the margins of their scripts, but even so, it was challenging. If a scene was written in blank verse (usually iambic pentameter), Shakespeare's syntax was often a function of the meter. This results in a kind of brilliant shorthand. A simple example—this is Hermia, in *A Midsummer Night's Dream (MND)*:

> *Dark night, that from the eye his function takes,*
> *The ear more quick of apprehension makes;*

They're in the forest, at night; finally discovering Lysander, very relieved, Hermia repeats the truism about how when it's dark you can't see, but you can hear better. (Inevitably, a student new to Shakespeare would respond, "Well, why didn't he say that?") But the syntax is shifted around, in order to meet the demands of the meter. And also, of course, to be poetry—heightened emotion certainly, but along with it that characteristic Shakespearean touch: starting with *"dark night,"* we could be going anywhere—and then the night steals/obscures something— what is it? The mini-mystery, created then resolved, is so typical of how he operates—and how, as previously noted, his re-arrangements engage and excite the brain.

A more complicated example (Hamlet, on his way to confront his mother):

> *I will speak daggers to her, but use none;*
> *My tongue and soul in this be hypocrites;*
> *How in my words soever she be shent,*
> *To give them seals never, my soul, consent!*

"Shent" meaning "rebuked"; "To give them seals"—that is, to act on my words. However harshly I rebuke my mother, I will do her no violence. Notice the separation of "How" and "soever" to fit the meter, and the reversal of normal word order in the last line. The twisted words also reveal the inner ambivalence—tongue vs. soul—that governs Hamlet's behavior at this point. And as in the previous example, putting the verbs at the ends of the lines strengthens the impact.

Another thing that proved puzzling to many students, especially early on, was the seemingly cursory way Shakespeare dealt with plot. In *MND*, Oberon and Titania fight bitterly over her changeling child, and Titania vows never to give the boy up—*"Not for thy fairy kingdom!"* she yells at Oberon. Later on, in the forest, for no apparent reason, she hands the child over. Like several others, Demetrius is enchanted with a magical flower. But although the others are dis-enchanted with another herb, Demetrius is not. Is he changed forever? Did Shakespeare forget? Was it deliberate? Again, Hamlet's true age, and how much time passes during the events of the play, how he and Horatio just happen to be in the cemetery at the right time to witness Ophelia's mysterious burial, Hamlet's escape from the pirates—all these and more are never completely accounted for. Most confusing of all was the central pivot of *Much Ado About Nothing*: Hero's acceptance, in the end, of Claudio as a husband after he has publicly humiliated her at the altar. The fact that explanations for these supposed lapses existed (albeit sometimes overly legalistic and/or complex) didn't cut much ice with teenagers. As they discovered over time, Shakespeare was nothing if not infinitely mysterious.

And if this infinite mystery was not a factor in their enthusiasm at the beginning of our experience, it soon became one. After all, to take the best example first, there really is ultimately no explaining the "final meaning" of *Hamlet*. We performed it five times over the years, and each time it was a different play. Macbeth becomes a psychopath, and yet he has some of the most beautiful lines in the entire canon, and part of the appeal of that play is the tug within us between horror and self-acceptance. The ability to sustain a certain kind of cognitive dissonance—holding contradictory ideas—in art, and education, and life, is widely recognized as a step toward both maturity and creativity. It's also, I'm convinced, the only way to understand Shakespeare.

As I said before, most of this was of little practical concern to students. They were challenged by the language, and sometimes confused by the plots. Somehow, after months of reading, discussion, and rehearsals, they always seemed to get it.

> *Drama and Shakespeare have brought me to a whole new world. When I was onstage, I finally felt like me.*

> *I didn't really know who Shakespeare was and how important he was. The play taught me how Shakespeare felt and what he thought, and the kind of magic that can come from a person's heart.*

> *Drama and Shakespeare have given me confidence and hope. I'm MUCH different than I was in September.*

> *I learned that school can be fun, not a torture chamber. I feel more confident with Shakespeare, and it's given me a new insight on language.*

> *I have never felt as alive as when I was crawling behind miserable lovers [as Puck], fighting over Ophelia's body, or twisting the knife of guilt into Leontes.*

> *I learned that Shakespeare wrote in riddles. That in Much Ado you had to listen to the conversation to understand*

that it's NOT "much ado about nothing," but a play about looking and seeing.

No matter what a person's acting was like before, it always improves when they do Shakespeare.

I've gotten so much out of it. I've expanded my vocabulary, experienced the lives of so many people. If I hadn't started doing Shakespeare, I would probably be leading a stupid, boring life. Shakespeare has done so much for me, I can't even name all the reasons why. I'm so thankful I came here to get the chance to put on Shakespeare's incredible masterpieces.

I'm not who I used to be [after being Hamlet]. *Not after Puck, or Ophelia, Hermia, Bottom, or any of the others have I felt like this. I, myself, don't even know what this means yet, but I feel different. I actually cried after the performance. Not because it was over, but for something deeper than that. Thank you. I won't forget.*

Shakespeare has helped me understand about new words and stories. He helped me advance in acting, and experience how it feels to be a different person.

Shakespeare has opened a new door—a whole window, maybe—to a new way of acting. Acting is not just Wind in the Willows or Cinderella now. It's like stepping into a new world.

Shakespeare has given me a family and a whole new life to look forward to. It has opened my eyes and made life seem so much better than before.

I loved stepping onto the stage. Into Scotland. Becoming evil. Becoming Lady Macbeth. I love the way Shakespeare writes the words so that they sink into your soul.

*It has meant a lot to me. Before I started doing Shakespeare,
I thought he was just a dead white guy. But he's not, because
he lives on through his words. Drama has not changed me,
it has "translated" me. Life now feels like a walking dream.*

*Drama and Shakespeare have meant everything to me. They
have opened me up as a person, and made me more confident
that I can do anything I set my heart to.*

*Doing Shakespeare has opened my mind to new things. It
has made me see in a new light. It has taught me to work with
my class—no, family—because it is so powerful we have to
work together to make it work. Doing Shakespeare helps me
connect with the past and know it. Also, his words are true,
even though they were written so long ago. They tell about
what is going on in the world right now. Doing Shakespeare
has helped me connect with people I would not have otherwise,
and they have become my friends. Before doing this, I fought
more with people. Now I know we can work together, and I
love that! And Shakespeare is timeless, and by doing Shakespeare it has made me a little more deep.*

*I never thought I could do Shakespeare, I thought it would
be too confusing to understand and memorize, but I found
out that it's easy. It's fun and it's cool.*

*Drama and Shakespeare have given me more than I thought
possible. Together, they save friendships, stop quarrels, almost
anything bad in the way of interacting with people. When
Shakespeare wrote these fabulous plays, he created a living
and feeling thing of great and wonderful power.*

*It's meant everything to me. I can't live without Shakespeare.
Without it I am nothing. Shakespeare has given me life.*

*It's the most inspirational art that was ever made. This is how
art can save lives. In a way it has saved me—I am a whole
new person.*

You can drop all the bad things that are happening in your life and become Dogberry, or Hero. It's a wonderful thing. And Shakespeare. God has blessed us. Shakespeare is so Shakespeare, there are no words to describe it. It's so magical it just changes you.

Hero was a really great part because she's so dramatic. Margaret was another great part because she's so witty. It's meant a lot to me. I love Shakespeare. The words are so elaborate. Much Ado had such magic.

Shakespeare has transformed me. When you do Shakespeare, you become a different person. Maybe it's the beautiful poetic language. It's everything about it!! SHAKESPEARE RULES!!

Shakespeare is one of the greatest people who ever lived. And you can't just "do" Shakespeare. You have to live, breathe, eat, and sleep it.

My first impression was, this is Shakespeare, this is difficult, kids shouldn't do this. Then I saw the fifth scene onstage. I saw comedy, I saw romance, and trickery. In less than 10 minutes, I found Benedick a kindred soul.

Shakespeare has meant so so so so so much! It has given me a new door of light to explore. I wish I could just hug Shakespeare and say thank you so much, you have changed my vision completely.

"*Shakespeare has transformed me.*" This is a book about transformation, about how words written 400 years ago changed my life and the lives of my students. There were moments during our performances, moments I waited for, when certain lines were uttered onstage that always gave me that same "tingle" referred to earlier by an amazing sixth-grader. Here are just a few of dozens:

The childing autumn, angry winter, change
Their wonted liveries, and the mazed world,
By their increase, now knows not which is which:
And this same progeny of evils comes
From our debate, from our dissension;
We are their parents and original.
                    – Titania, *MND*

Now the hungry lion roars,
And the wolf behowls the moon;
Whilst the heavy ploughman snores,
All with weary task fordone.
Now the wasted brands do glow,
Whilst the screech-owl, screeching loud,
Puts the wretch that lies in woe
In remembrance of a shroud.
                    – Puck, *MND*

True is it that we have seen better days,
And have with holy bell been knolled to church
And sat at good men's feasts and wiped our eyes
Of drops that sacred pity hath engendered:
And therefore sit you down in gentleness
And take upon command what help we have
That to your wanting may be ministered.
                    – Duke Senior, *As You Like It*

But this rough magic
I here abjure, and, when I have required
Some heavenly music, which even now I do,
To work mine end upon their senses that
This airy charm is for, I'll break my staff,
Bury it certain fathoms in the earth,
And deeper than did ever plummet sound
I'll drown my book.
                    – Prospero, *The Tempest*

Lay her in the earth:
And from her fair and unpolluted flesh
May violets spring! I tell thee, churlish priest,
A ministering angel shall my sister be,
When thou liest howling!
                    – Laertes, *Hamlet*

What was it about these passages, and so many others, that made them so powerfully affecting to me? It's obvious that Shakespeare found a way to connect the emotional lives of his characters directly to our deepest feelings. More than that, it was the way he used a unique combination of powerful language, poetic rhythms (even in prose), a mysterious, mind-expanding syntax, and brilliant images to slap us awake from the ordinary world, and deliver us into hidden realities.

It was no surprise, then, that my students felt the same way about the words they said and heard onstage. Something mysterious and intensely meaningful was happening, and it was changing us. Like Bottom transformed, we had fallen under the hypnotic spell of *"a spirit of no common rate."*

Ophelia and Hamlet. [*Hamlet*]

New Friends and Stranger Companies

How did this happen? How did all the crazy things Al Cullum promised me in *Shake Hands with Shakespeare,* and more, actually come to pass? Some of it was serendipity, a harmonic convergence of the right idea with the right kids at the right time. The most important factor was commitment—the willingness of students and parents to dedicate large amounts of time and energy to facilitating rehearsals, performances, and the associated activities that sustained the whole process.

Once my class became dedicated to doing serious drama, after the first year, it became a tradition. Younger students, some of whom were siblings of the kids in my class, began to look forward to trying Shakespeare for themselves. They noticed that the process was challenging and exciting, and so it came to take on some aspects of a rite of passage. And as the tradition of doing Shakespeare began to repeat, it began to accrue various rituals and sub-traditions, until it eventually emerged as a kind of culture of its own.

One of the things we started doing very early on was making a yearly pilgrimage to Ashland, Oregon, home of the Oregon Shakespeare Festival (OSF). Even after students graduated out of my class, many continued to come to Ashland every summer. Ashland is a beautiful place, especially nationally-famous Lithia Park, which became our home away from home. The park is adjacent to the Festival, just below the replica Elizabethan playhouse, and the kids would often spend the day there while we waited for performances to begin. Hours-long frisbee marathons on the "Feast of Will Lawn" became both a bonding ritual and an acid test of an actor's endurance. For many years, parents would even bring huge loads of costumes down, so we could do "Scenes from Shakespeare"—as they were advertised on the handbills we passed out—featuring "The Options Players/ World Famous in Kitsap County, Washington."

Best of all, and the focus of the long trip, were the plays. When we started going to OSF, very few of the students had ever seen a live Shakespeare play. The impact of seeing something we ourselves had done performed on the Elizabethan stage was enormous. The very first year we went, we had just finished performing *Hamlet*. In Ashland, the first play the students saw, in the Elizabethan theater, was *Hamlet*. The effect was electric. There was an excited whispered buzzing between scenes, and after the play their impressions spilled out.

> *It was amazing...I am incredibly jealous! I remember standing on the stage before the show and thinking, Wow!...It was sooo beautiful, lovely, it was nothing like I imagined...The lights, the colors, it was an incredible experience...Awesome! ...It was so beautiful! When we went in, I just stared. I (along with everyone else, I'm guessing) was tempted to jump up onstage and belt out my lines..."Wow! Oh my God!" were my first words. I couldn't believe my eyes. It was everything I had imagined and even more...The set had a perfect feel to it...I loved the blocking ... Every way they moved there was light on them...They used every part of the stage. The costumes were neat because they kind of described the character's personality. Also, the way they didn't use a curtain, and there was always something happening onstage...It was similar to the Mel Gibson version...I liked how everything they did was exaggerated...Ophelia was so emotional! And no one missed a cue ...Really liked the relationship between Ophelia and Laertes...I liked the Queen, how it made her drunk, and how she came on and said "There is a willow...."*
> *...It was interesting how after the Queen's speech about Ophelia's death she started laughing and then turned it into crying... Hamlet was really strong and big, compared to the King who appeared small and evil. The King seemed to be scared, but he wasn't scared enough to give up what he killed for...I was really*

impressed by the scene between Hamlet and Ophelia.
It was really effective how physical they were.

Thanks to determined parents, the kids had great seats—most sat right in the front two rows. In Act I, Scene two, Hamlet entered from a vomitorium behind their seats; I'll never forget seeing the looks on their faces when he spoke his first line from the audience—*"A little more than kin, and less than kind."*—and their heads turned in surprise. They were stunned, and felt as if they were actually inside the play itself. That moment alone was a breakthrough, a kind of validation of our whole school year. They were hooked.

Another bonding ritual which we started very early was the casting ceremony. Auditions in our class were standard, but very informal. The rule was that you could audition for any three roles you wanted, solo or with helpers. I used the hints I got from these auditions, plus the list of "What Roles I Want" from each student—plus a healthy dose of acquired knowledge about each student's capabilities, social/emotional needs, etc.—to put together the cast lists (I used two or three casts for each play, so that each student got at least one major role). Before the ceremony, I would have prepared special fancy "scrolls" for each student, detailing which roles in which casts I had given them.

As the time neared, older students would make the stage ready. The curtains would be drawn, to isolate us from other kids and parents coming and going into the room (the back of my classroom served as the Options Program parent HQ). In the middle of the stage, "Howard" (Bottom's ass-head, named by one of the first *MND* casts) would be placed in the position of honor—our mascot/talisman/protector. Then, the big moment. As anxious and excited as on Christmas morning, the kids seated themselves in a circle around the edges of the stage, boy-girl alternately as our house rule required, many (sometimes the whole group) holding hands in nervousness.

Before I started calling names and handing out scrolls, though, as the ritual demanded I asked them, "What are the things we always remember now?" And the answers came back quickly from the older students, who had been through this several times: *"Don't brag." "If you didn't get the part you wanted, it's still going to be a part you'll like—we've been*

23

there." "There are no small parts, only small salaries." (a bad joke courtesy of a great dad who had been a longtime union stagehand) *"Make sure everyone in the class feels important and supported." "Younger guys—your turn will come."* (a reminder that since kids were in my class for 2 years, they would get bigger parts next year) *"And if you don't think it's fair, don't blame the person who got the part you wanted. Blame the director!"*

Finally I handed out the scrolls. Now was the time for the superstitious ones to kiss Howard for luck. Some kids—the younger ones—opened theirs right away, they couldn't stand the suspense. Older kids, making a show of their nonchalance (and knowing they would get something good), would wait until all the scrolls were handed out, and we went around the circle asking each person to read what roles they got in which casts. Then they would calmly unroll their scroll for the first time and read it—for themselves and for everyone.

Much excitement. Sometimes, a few tears, questions for the director; once in a great while, some extended sulking. True to their words, the older students made a point of supporting kids who were disappointed. Soon, all were happily (more or less) marking up their scripts with yellow highlighters, and we were on our way. Including, always, much merriment about who was "married" to whom, who the lovers were, and who was whose father/mother. And much pointing out by the older students, in response, that it was the characters that had these relationships, NOT you, and please, try to be more professional about it.

> *I'll never forget, behind those curtains, the donkey-head that I wore once. Unrolling my scroll. Puck. Hermia.*

> *I remember when everybody got their parts and everybody was screaming they were so happy. When I saw "Bottom" I was SO excited that this year I would be the one to make the audience laugh.*

> *I remember auditioning, with everyone around you. When I was saying the lines the room seemed empty. I felt like I was the only person in the room but I was also scared. All eyes felt like mirrors. And kissing the donkey before getting my part. Slowly unrolling*

the paper to see what you got. A part that you would play with your classmates—no, your family—for the next four months. Disappointment mixed with excitement. A sadness that this would be your last play, mixed with enjoyment.

I remember getting our parts: picking the flowers, unrolling the scrolls, kissing Howard for luck, and putting together the puzzle, of everyone trying to fit together.

I was disappointed that I didn't get the part I wanted, but I tried not to show it and resolved to do the best I could at the parts given me.

When I unrolled my paper to see, "Congratulations! You are Macbeth!" every feeling of joy, amazement, happiness went through my head.

I was sooooo nervous all day. I really wanted Rosaline! [Love's Labor's Lost] Then we got onstage with the curtains closed, and soon I got my part. So I opened it, and it was Rosaline! The butterflies in my stomach settled down. I was so happy! The rest of the day I kept checking my piece of paper to see if it was really true.

I remember sitting in a circle behind the curtain, waiting to find out. And when I did I got the most wonderful laughing sensation.

Trying out for Hermione [The Winter's Tale]. I was shaking so bad I scared myself—so I shook more. This role. I had never wanted a part so bad, I really loved Hermione and wanted to make her how I imagined her, or at least show people how cool she was. In other plays it was just acting. I really felt this one.

I wasn't very happy with the parts I got, but it turned out they were the best parts I ever played.

The two most important bonding activities we did, and the keys to this entire adventure, were our processing circles and our trust-building routine. The latter deserves its own chapter, and I will discuss it at length later on. Circles were part of trust-building, but also different, and just as essential in several ways.

Before and after every rehearsal, and after every performance, if at all possible, the actors and crew sat in a circle onstage. Before rehearsals, circles were a time to go over what scenes and ideas we were working on. They were also a time for questions about the play—blocking, difficult lines, possible cuts, and so on. Also, it was during circle time that any friction among the cast was brought up. Our motto was "Fix the problem, not the blame," and for the most part we stuck to it. If it became apparent that a conflict was deeper and in need of more attention, I would use older students as peer mediators. Most of the time, the atmosphere of the circle was quite conducive to problem-solving.

The most important purpose of the circle was to give the actors a chance to compliment each other. No criticism was allowed, except under special circumstances (if something had gone badly wrong during a show, we allowed "constructive criticism"). Another rule was that no one should be left out. And no one liked to hear something along the lines of, "You were really good," so there was strong internal pressure from the start for praise to be specific "I statements"—"I liked the way you _____."

From the very first time we did it, the compliment circle proved very effective at bringing the kids together. For one thing, everyone loves to hear their efforts praised. Beginning actors wanted to know that they were part of the group, that they were contributing to the progress of the play. What was especially effective, and older students became quite good at this—after all, it helped everyone—was when someone noticed a specific way in which you had improved, or "moved it up," as we said. "I really liked the way you talked louder when you were Moonshine, it was way better than yesterday." This, coming from a peer or older actor, was almost guaranteed to have a multiplying effect on the group: everyone wanted to hear it about themselves, and everyone wanted to able to say it. After all, as the ages-old bumper sticker above our classroom door said, *Everyone Does Better When Everyone Does Better.*

The compliment circle was also a way for the kids to have a group conversation about the way we were doing the play. William Blake famously wrote, "Damn braces. Bless relaxes."—and it was never so true as in our circles. Compliments had a way of giving kids freedom—freedom to question the other actors who were playing the same role, to question their own interpretations and ideas, to suggest new ways for the whole group to block certain scenes, to ask for help during certain key moments.

If someone with a smaller role was being ignored, all it took was brief eye contact with an older student, and a nod in the right direction, for a compliment to be thought of and spoken. Older students were keenly aware of how important this was.

Compliment circles were very energizing! The ordinary dynamic of our classroom was sometimes divisive: older students tended to hang together at independent study times, as did younger or newer students. Teacher-directed mixing for group activities happened a lot, but nothing beat the compliment circles for promoting cohesiveness. We all wanted the play to work, and after a few months of circles and trust-building, we knew that success depended on how well we could learn to work together. No matter what happened during class, or after school, an hour of positive feedback had the power to re-weave the connections among us, and make us stronger.

photo by Isabel Gates

Bottom. [*A Midsummer Night's Dream*]

To Bring Moonlight into a Chamber

As our way of doing Shakespeare began to develop its own rituals and culture, we began moving into a new kind of classroom experience. What a difference it made, to have something serious and substantial that we were all working to achieve. Something to practice, discuss, and bond around. Something that was exciting, and totally worth our time and energy. Above all, something that was incredibly fun for each of us.

And so, we began to come under Shakespeare's brilliant spell; and the one play that most helped to facilitate it all was *A Midsummer Night's Dream*. I had always been fascinated by *MND*. In 1984, I watched my oldest son play Snug/the Lion in a Williamette University production in Salem, Oregon, where I first saw Puck punctuate the line *"Give me your hands"* by casting glitter into the audience. In the early 90s, I saw a seamless OSF production of *MND* that included a disabled actor in a wheelchair, who played Snout/Wall effortlessly and memorably. *MND* is such a perfect choice for kids. It's a comedy—toward which middle-school students are naturally inclined. It has the best balance of male/female roles in all of Shakespeare. It not only tolerates but requires amateurish acting in many scenes (the adventures of the "mechanicals"). It's otherworldly and mysterious. It has a multiplicity of "lead" roles (the four lovers, Bottom, Quince, Titania, Oberon, Puck, and Theseus all have big parts). It has singing and dancing. It has a hilarious catfight between two of the female leads. And it has the funniest scene—and all-time favorite scene of young actors everywhere—in all of Shakespeare, *"The Most Lamentable Comedy and Most Cruel Death of Pyramus and Thisby."* Best of all, students loved it.

Hermia's angry face coming up from behind the sofa—and the fear in Helena's eyes was so real. The lights. The fairy dance. The smell of make-up and flowers as I call my fairies. The taste of excitement as you wait to go on. The sounds of the catfight. And Titania's strong voice, and the clear true voices of fairies singing, and Puck romping through the woods looking for mischief. The feeling that all will turn out okay in the end! The feeling of a job well done, of unity in the class. The love that happens! And knowing that you can't go wrong!

Over the course of fifteen years, we did this play eight times, and each production was different. Different ages students—from nine-year-olds to fifteen-year-olds. Different script lengths and arrangements. Different cuts in characters and scenes. Different themes. But the central fact of the play, its magical ability to transform actors and audiences, was always a constant. This is another huge advantage of doing *MND:* its pliability. It is almost infinitely adaptable and changeable, but it always retains that wonderful essential magic.

Four character sets make up the world of *MND*, and each set has its own kind of appeal to, and possibilities for, student actors. Duke Theseus, his bride-to-be Hippolyta, his Master of the Revels Philostrate, and his friend Egeus (Hermia's father) make up what are commonly (or royally?) called "the royals." Hermia, her best friend Helena, her frustrated suitor Demetrius, and her boyfriend Lysander are "the lovers." Ordered by Theseus to marry Demetrius or die, Hermia flees to the forest with Lysander; Helena and Demetrius follow, in pursuit. Meanwhile, a group of Athenian craftsmen has been called together by their leader, Peter Quince the carpenter, to prepare a play ("Pyramus and Thisby") for the Duke's wedding; Bottom the weaver wants to play all of the roles, but they are ultimately divided among him, Snug the joiner, Snout the tinker, Flute the bellows-mender, and Starveling the tailor. Philostrate calls these men "rude mechanicals," but we always called them simply "the workers." And surrounding all, the fairies: Titania the Queen; her handmaids First Fairy, Cobweb, Mustardseed, and Peaseblossom; Oberon the King, and his retainer Robin Goodfellow, or Puck.

The Faery Realm, and especially the three key roles, had a tremendous appeal for many students—not surprising, of course, but underneath the archetypal attraction, several things were going on. One was music and dance. Depending on what version we did, the fairies had four or five songs and three or four dances; kids who were naturally musical, or who were simply attracted to the pageantry, gravitated to these roles. Another factor was group acting: Titania's retinue were always together, and a shy actor sometimes found it easier to get started in drama as a member of this group. Then there was the appeal of being invisible to mortals. Oberon and Puck, and sometimes the other fairies, remain onstage while the lovers are fighting. Puck, of course, is the invisible instigator of much of the conflict. So many kids loved the idea of being able to shadow the mortals onstage, and maybe even make fun of them. Invisibility, the ultimate mask!

The appeal of using magic was fundamental. Oberon, Titania, and Puck all have it, and use it. What adolescent could resist this kind of power over the poor, stupid humans? Allied with this was the appeal of control. Fairies were pure Id, and the idea that your wildest impulses could be in charge of the adult world, even if only briefly, was a great draw.

Faery was a world outside of logic, a world governed by intense emotions: Titania's righteous anger, Oberon's revenge, and Puck's reckless mischief-making. Whatever they did, fairies never had to explain or justify it—especially Puck. Not only was Puck never truly contrite, he actually reveled in the chaos he created. For a young person on the edge of puberty, what's not to love?

> *I remember feeling like First Fairy all the time. Seeing the anger in M- and E- when they were Titania. The sound of all the fairies singing together—and sounding like fairies.*

> *The lights were so great, I couldn't see the audience very well, so I thought I actually WAS Puck. It was fun. Hee hee hee! I - LOVE - IT!*

> *It is just amazing, every time you go onstage, you get into your character more and more. I never thought I could do that but I did it and I loved it, just feeling like a fairy. Once performances started I was soooo nervous, I had so many*

butterflies in my stomach, but when I got onstage I had so much fun. I just went into that other world and had a blast. I thought to myself, you are not you, you are First Fairy.

My most vivid memory is Puck's entrance on the first night, with the wild make-up on.

I have never been more comfortable onstage in my life [he was Oberon]. *The connection that Puck and I had was perfect. I loved being onstage. It was like we would throw some vibes through our words and actions to the audience, and they would respond with laughter and toss those vibes back, and we just played catch with some vibes for an hour and a half.*

I remember hearing Titania call out/scream at the beginning of the play and it sounded wild, like something out of the wilderness. I remember seeing Puck crawl out of the grave like something out of a dream. All the fairies onstage glittering in the light, they all looked so ethereal and beautiful.

The fairies doing all our new things onstage, thinking them up as we went along. All of us, just making it work.

I'll always remember watching the process, watching the actors and myself [as Puck] *grow as our characters and ourselves. And taking off my top hat at the end of the performance, saying those last few lines, and feeling it all disappear into the sky.*

How there was always total silence while Titania was saying the "forgeries of jealousy."

I remember Oberon onstage: angry, waiting for me [Puck].

I remember feeling like First Fairy, and NOT myself, and I loved that feeling. I will never forget it. I was not saying passages, I was saying what she was saying.

I'm a lot more like Titania and Puck than I realized. Parts of me want to be noble and have that holier-than-thou feeling. The other part is sneaky and wild. Puck does have a dark side. I feel like I was able to be consumed by that.

I knew I could do a lot of things as Puck, but actually doing it really enhanced my capabilities.

Being Puck made me think, you can have fun, but you should still be trustworthy.

I remember sitting on an unsuspecting kindergartner as Puck, and having little people squeal in laughter when I tried to find a place to sit.

People letting loose. Inside me, tears coming through my eyes unexpected. Freedom, lots of freedom. Sounds of little kids laughing at my every move.

I remember when I was Puck, and in that last speech of the play I looked up into the lights and thought, "I will never forget this," and then throwing the glitter.

Being onstage [as Puck] and feeling the rush of the first performance like everything is magical, it feels like dancing with fairies. How can that not change me?

The four lovers had a different kind of allure. Everyone loved the catfight scene, of course. Having a knock-down, drag-out showdown confrontation with your best-friend-for-life, in which all the issues and hard feelings you had both ignored for years were suddenly and violently exposed—wow! This was the scene we practiced the most, and the one everyone always stopped to watch. No matter how tight the blocking was supposed to be, something new always happened.

The catfight scene! Seeing Hermia being tossed around—I had to close my eyes!…I remember pain. Suffering. Agony. All from the catfight!…I remember vaulting over the sofa to tackle Hermia…And when Hermia said, "You, mistress, all this is because of you!"…That unsatisfiable anger during the catfight scene, wanting to get something I could not have …The way Helena was always so attached to Demetrius, it made me laugh a lot …Jumping on Helena!…The puppy-dog look on Demetrius's face when he was in love with Helena …The time when I threw Hermia on top of Demetrius, everybody said "Oooh" at the same time, but Demetrius was a good sport and kept the play going…The catfight scene started with us standing motionless looking at our scripts, It ended with people hurtling offstage…And Lysander and Demetrius doing the "sissy-fighting" with their hands…I remember when Helena and I were behind the chairs, "fighting." Our hands and feet would be madly thumping on the floor and we would be kicking and screaming—but whenever we looked at each other we would be smiling as big as we could…In performance I had just said my line and no one else knew what to say, so it was silent for a few minutes—then Helena yelled, "Don't touch me!"…Doing the catfight scene was so intense, it brought the play up to a new level. It was awesome!…A PERFECT catfight!…When Hermia said, "How low am I?" and Lysander said, "Very very very low, uh huh."…And when Helena SAT on Demetrius, and then Hermia pulled her hair— and then Helena carefully placing Demetrius and Lysander between herself and Hermia…The way the boys fought over Helena's coat…When Hermia tied my shoelaces together! I really liked that part, and a lot of people laughed…The screaming in the catfight scene. Being thrown around as Lysander. Hiding from Hermia, then being dragged by her…When Helena picked little Demetrius up and threw him across the

> *stage, and then got me (Hermia) in a headlock...When Hermia*
> *said, "Reach into thine eyes" and then stopped and then jumped!*
> *...Helena putting Demetrius in front of her—and then Deme-*
> *trius putting Lysander in front of him! Helena stomping on both*
> *boys' feet at the same time...We never did it the same way twice,*
> *but it always worked out.*

Eventually, usually without life-threatening injuries, this conflict is resolved—by exhaustion, mostly.

Nearby, in another part of the forest, Oberon's revenge on sleeping Titania is being played out. He has enchanted her so that she will fall madly in love with the first creature she sees, and our Oberons loved saying these magic words:

> *What thou seest when thou dost wake,*
> *Do it for thy true-love take,*
> *Love and languish for his sake:*
> *Be it ounce, or cat, or bear,*
> *Pard, or boar with bristled hair,*
> *In thy eye that shall appear*
> *When thou wakest, it is thy dear:*
> *Wake when some vile thing is near.*

"Ounce" was a bad French translation of the Latin word for lynx; a "pard" was a leopard. But poor Titania isn't lucky enough to fall for either of these noble beasts, and all the Pucks got a huge charge out of telling Oberon what happened:

> *When in that moment, so it came to pass,*
> *Titania waked and straightway loved an ass.*

And each one took the opportunity to insert a wonderfully pregnant pause after the word "loved."

The ass, of course, was Bottom the Weaver. (Actually. Bottom is only a figurative ass, since his "bottom" half is still a man.) Transformed by Puck in the middle of the workers' play rehearsal, Bottom sings to drive away his fears, and in so doing wakes Titania, and it's love at first enchanted sight. Particularly for younger audiences, the sight of the beautiful fairy queen going ga-ga over a poor worker with Howard fixed on his head was completely hilarious, and our actors played the mismatch for all it was worth. It soon became a tradition for the actor playing Bottom to affect a slight donkey-overbite, and after every one of Titania's bizarre compliments (*"Thou art as wise as thou art beautiful"*), to bashfully reply, *"Awwwwww . . . not so neither"*—and then to keep repeating that sound, until the incongruity put even the actors in danger of losing it.

Many students wanted to play Bottom. Besides being *"the one to make the audience laugh,"* Bottom never loses his dignity. He is totally and completely self-possessed, accepting everything that happens to him with equanimity, a perfect Eternal Child. When he wakes from his dream-within-a-dream, the romance with Titania, even without exactly remembering it he knows the dream has been hugely significant, and he thinks of a way to immortalize it:

> *I will get Peter Quince to write a ballad of this dream:*
> *it shall be called Bottom's Dream, because it hath no bottom.*

The dream, that is, (1) has no Bottom the Weaver, since he was some-one/something else; (2) has no foundation, being only a dream; but also, and most importantly, (3) is so deep and mysterious as to be bottomless. Like the wonderful world of *MND* itself—and, as several recent critics have asserted, like the whole of William Shakespeare's work.

The last scene ties together all the different threads, and it is one the students and our audiences always looked forward to with eager antici-pation. The Duke throws a wedding party, the reunited lovers attend, the workers perform "Pyramus and Thisby," and the fairies end the play by blessing the newly-married couples. Bottom's performance as Pyramus was, inevitably, the highlight of our every performance. The B-movie scenario ("Pyramus and Thisby" was a kind of parody version of Romeo and Juliet), the stock characters, and the painfully archaic language make it irresistible. Bottom/Pyramus's dying lines are the best example:

> *O wherefore, Nature, didst thou lions frame?*
> *Since lion vile hath here deflowered my dear:*

Which is—no, no—which was the fairest dame
That lived, that loved, that liked, that looked with cheer.
Come, tears, confound;
Out, sword, and wound
The pap of Pyramus;
Ay, that left pap,
Where heart doth hop:

[Stabs himself]
Thus die I, thus, thus, thus.
Now am I dead,
Now am I fled;
My soul is in the sky:
Tongue, lose thy light;
Moon take thy flight:
Now die, die, die, die, die.

And die our actor heroes did—over and over again, by their swords, by self-made fires, by explosions, by gas, electrocution, guillotine, by strangling themselves with their own intestines (yes, it's true)—in short, in any way they could think of that hadn't yet been done onstage by an Options actor. This is the supreme opportunity in all of Shakespeare to improvise within a controlled situation, and our Bottoms loved taking advantage of it. *"I will never forget lying awake at night before the last performance, trying to think of new ways to die,"* remembered one.

Upstage left, in this scene, sit the royals and the lovers, sipping pretend wine in fancy goblets and making scathing remarks about the quality of the play before them. Downstage right, the workers are giving it their all, under the direction of an increasingly embarrassed Peter Quince—who, when Pyramus messes up the second line of his speech (above) by saying "deflowered," corrects him by yelling "de-VOURED!" All is slapstick and mirth until the very end, when Shakespeare inserts one of his characteristically perfect touches. Young Flute the bellows-mender, playing Thisby (the parody Juliet), enters to find her lover dead (but sometimes still twitching gamely…). The first part of her ensuing lament is still more awful sentimentality, and the noble audience is groaning with impatience.

Then, all of a sudden, there is a pause. Thisby stops, assumes a quiet dignity we didn't know was in her, carefully wipes off her hideously-applied lipstick, and beautifully—like a real actress, not like an Athenian worker—recites her final lines, entrusting herself to the Fates:

> *O Sisters Three,*
> *Come, come to me,*
> *With hands as pale as milk;*
> *Lay them in gore,*
> *Since you have shore*
> *With shears his thread of silk.*
> *Tongue, not a word:*
> *Come, trusty sword;*
> *Come, blade, my breast imbrue:*
>
> *[Stabs herself]*
> *And, farewell, friends;*
> *Thus Thisby ends:*
> *Adieu, adieu, adieu.*

Several of our Thisbys actually managed to shed tears at this point, but even when they didn't, the effect of Thisby's new-found dignity was quite powerful. The chastened lovers were abashed—and it became another tradition for Hippolyta to rise, walk over in the silence when Thisby pauses, and give her a scarf to help with the lipstick. The mood has completely changed. The kids loved this moment, this small triumph of the powerless over their rulers, and even though Flute/Thisby was a relatively small part, there was always a huge demand for it.

And then of course, this being Shakespeare, the mood changes again. I played the same low note on the piano softly 12 times, and Theseus declares

> *The iron tongue of midnight hath told twelve:*
> *Lovers, to bed; 'tis almost fairy time.*

The stage empties, and the lights go down for the entry of Oberon, Titania, and their train of fairies. Oberon and Titania lead a solemn song and dance, anoint each fairy with *"field-dew consecrate,"* and finally, give the palace and its occupants their parting blessing. Lights down again, then Puck takes the small spotlight for the final lines.

We started with Al Cullum's 20-page abridgment of *MND*, but the next time we did it I expanded the script, adding in more lines from the original. The year after that, because the kids had been to OSF and wanted still more, I expanded it even further. Now we were up to 45 pages, and a performance time of an hour and a half. After adding more Shakespeare plays to our repertoire, though, that script seemed outdated. So, for the fourth version, we went up to 55 pages, about 3/4 of the original play, and almost two hours of performance time. Each time, the kids proved up to the challenge—and I had to admit, with more material, it was much easier to equalize the casting.

One version we did had a circus theme, *MND* as "The Athens Family Circus." The royals were the ringmasters, the lovers were the temperamental acrobatic troupe, the workers were clowns, and the fairies were gypsy-esque hangers-on. This actually worked out pretty well—the props and costumes were very easy (and spectacular), and the traditional mystery and excitement of a circus added to the effect.

Another year, several parents painted us a striking urban cityscape backdrop, complete with skyscrapers. This contemporary version hinged on a pending merger between "The Athens Co." (Theseus) and Hippolyta's firm, "Amazon.Com" (yes, it was a horrible pun). The play opened high up in an unfinished skyscraper; Theseus and Hippolyta are negotiating, but the lovers' quarrel interrupts them. Lysander explains his getaway plan to Hermia with an overhead projector and map of Athens—the lovers were spoiled yuppies, of course. The workers were a construction crew, trying to finish the building; and the fairies were hippies, "squatting" (illegally occupying) an unfinished floor. This version proved to be a little much—but the set was beautiful!

We made one final alteration to the script—I believe it was about five years in. After seeing a live performance somewhere—probably OSF, but I don't remember for sure—in which the first fairy scene became the first scene of the play, we all looked at each other and said—Yes! If your vision of *MND* is that Faery has the central place, and that the darkness and mystery of that world should set the tone for the whole story, sharpening the impact with strong contrast, then it made sense to change the scene order a bit. Was it okay? Was it still "Shakespearean"? I had some momentary doubts, but finally decided that if professionals thought it was okay, that was good enough for me! So we started opening the play with the confrontation between Puck and First Fairy, making it a real—slightly antagonistic—conflict, and punctuating it by setting First Fairy's beautiful long first speech to music—a melody that almost plagiarized "Light My Fire," with a medium-rock beat. We had some exceptional dance students those first few years, and one of them kept coming back to choreograph for us. Kicking the play off this way was a huge hit with the kids, and re-energized the whole thing. And as an added benefit, it engaged the audience immediately.

Audience response is naturally a big deal for student actors. The difference between night performances, mainly attended by parents, families, and friends, and daytime shows—in front of other students—was always noticeable. This was another reason why doing *MND* was such a huge boost to the growth of our theater troupe. Everyone loved it, every time; no matter what the quality of the show (in terms of readiness for the stage), audiences always got into it—especially kids. They might not completely understand the language, but they understood the story, and they loved the characters. Most of all, all audiences could tell that we understood it and were having fun with it—so they did too. The appeal of the fairies and magic; the hilarious shock of Bottom's transformation; the excitement of the catfight; and the foolishness and catharsis of the last scene—it never failed. *MND* soon became our signature piece.

I remember so well something a mom said to me after one of our first productions of *MND*. Sometimes we let younger kids in our program appear onstage as fairies, and this woman's daughter, a thrilled second-grader, had just finished her first performance as Peaseblossom. After the show, the little girl had quietly approached her mom and said, *"Mom, I finally feel like myself."*

> *MND has always been my favorite play to do. Without MND,*
> *something would just be missing. It makes me so happy, and*
> *we have such a great group of actors! Even though I have had*

the same parts before, it never gets old, and it's always really exciting. Long live MND!

It's the only thing going on right now that makes me really happy. It's one of my favorite Shakespeare plays—all the mistaken identity, action, and comedy just makes it fun.

I wish we could do it again and again and again. I had one of the best times of my life.

In other plays if you overact it ruins the play, but in MND it makes the play better!

This play has been different every time I have been in it. It changes the moment I get onstage…like a dream… honestly, I have no idea what is going to happen.

What helped me the most? MND itself helped me the most! It made me happy when nothing else would. I was excited to go every day.

How do you describe living in magic? Disconnected, but more connected to everyone else than ever. The day after the last performance, I was walking somewhere and felt lost, because I didn't know if I would feel this again.

MND taught me that the reality that almost everyone I know takes for granted—I am not so sure it is what we think. I doubt, I barely believe, in that reality. I do not believe it is my truth, at least. The way I feel about this is impossible to express, but the play, the words and what we did with them, has helped give it shape. If our reality is to be believed, nothing is what it seems….

It taught me that I can show someone imagination. That I can give someone a story that they can dream about. I can pour out thoughts that have not been thought about, and they will remember that they have been there.

I've never felt like I was truly a part of a group before, and it felt good, admittedly. We are a machine that is greater than the sum of all of its parts. I've never felt so loved or accepted as I did onstage. And that is no jest.

This play keeps me going. I wake up in the morning wondering what it's gonna be like today.

I first came into MND because I needed a way to escape "friends," school, girl scouts, swimming, and most of all, stress. I needed to get away. I have found out that MND is more than that—it's not just acting, it's being creative with everything you do. It's plain fun, and I love it. If I hadn't done MND, I probably would have become a mindless drone, and my spirit would have completely died. I needed MND.

MND is my way of letting out my emotions of the day: stress, anger, happiness—that kind of stuff.

It's like you're in a new world, and it's a fantastic world, it's so different and amazing.

I'll always remember being up there, with the lights baking me. It may not be that much now, but it will make SO much of a difference in the rest of my life.

Walking away, seeing it's over. Not being Helena. Nowhere to escape to. No world to live in.

I LOVE MND, it is an awesome, amazing play and I'm so glad we did it. I think doing it has changed me as a person. I feel more like a person in the world doing something more complete. Not a nobody, not just another person on planet Earth.

*MND changed my relationships with everyone, because of
trust and the fun we had. I feel like doing the play gave me a
life that is worthwhile. And I learned I don't have to keep in
my feelings.*

*I learned how to be an ass! (Joke!) But also, to not be so BIG
of an ass! I thought the play was extremely good, and my
strongest feeling about it is that I want to do it again, and
never stop.*

*When I think back on MND, I think of everybody getting
their parts. Then I think of the final bow, everybody onstage.
One smiling group. One smiling family . . . And farewell
friends, but MND does not end. It will live forever in our
hearts.*

Many contemporary productions do this play solely for laughs, and
as a "star turn" for the actors playing the lead roles, a chance for them
to do stand-up comedy. The fairies become Victorian caricatures, or
Disney-esque cartoon figures. Very rarely is Faery seriously dark and
otherworldly, and even a bit threatening to the human world. I'm with
David Young, whose book on *MND* is one of the best:

*Modern productions, stressing the non-demonic, have
seriously misrepresented the fairies as gauzy, fluttery
creatures with no more mystery or authority than butterflies. Something is lost by this. Oberon is not harmless,
he is a prince from the farthest steep of India, shadowy
and exotic. Titania is a powerful force—'The summer
still doth tend upon my state'—and Bottom is virtually
her prisoner. The marital disturbances of these beings
affect the weather and the natural cycles and result in
floods, droughts, and famines. Their benevolent presence
in the play serves to emphasize the comic context only if
they are recognized as potentially dangerous.*
                              –David Young, *Something of Great Constancy*

A Midsummer Night's Dream speaks directly to, and about, the unconscious. It is no accident that the counterpart to the forest of misrule is the city of Athens—a place of laws and human logic, where Hermia can be sentenced to exile or death for falling in love with the wrong person. *MND* is about the underside of that world: a place where we change without willing or knowing it; where love alters everything—and not always for the better; and where hidden emotions and secret desires come out to play, defying both logic and law.

Luckily, most middle-schoolers are not yet so advanced in the cynicism media teaches them that they cannot see *MND* for what it is—a door to a world where, as one student says above, "nothing is what it seems." Where people forget, and also remember. Where anything is possible.

> QUINCE
>> Well it shall be so. But there is two hard things; that is, to bring
>> the moonlight into a chamber; for, you know, Pyramus and
>> Thisby meet by moonlight.
>
> SNOUT
>> Doth the moon shine that night we play our play?
>
> BOTTOM
>> A calendar, a calendar! Look in the almanac; find out moonshine,
>> find out moonshine.
>
> QUINCE
>> Yes, it doth shine that night.
>
> BOTTOM
>> Why, then may you leave a casement of the great chamber
>> window, where we play, open, and the moon may shine in at
>> the casement.

Give Me Your Hands

Sometimes if you're very lucky, when you start a project that gets everyone involved and excited a kind of synergy happens. That is, the results prove to be somehow greater than the sum of the project's individual components. Students begin to feel engaged in a way that empowers them to be more creative and more expressive, and to participate more intensely in the classroom dynamic. Classroom discussions become more interesting and meaningful to more students. Group brainstorming and problem-solving improve. Play rehearsals are smoother.

This happened over and over when we started doing theater together, and it created an energy that was contagious. More parents began to be involved—for example, we began to get regular snacks at rehearsal breaks! Students' work in other areas of the curriculum began to get better, as they became more motivated and confident. Absenteeism dropped—kids were excited to be at school. And a few little things began to happen that were so perfectly synchronous with what we were doing as to seem more than mere coincidence.

During our first full year of this inspired madness, one of my colleagues mentioned a new book she had seen at the school library. It was a young adult novel called *King of Shadows,* by the famous children's author, Susan Cooper. Intrigued by her description, I checked the book out and read it overnight. The next day, at read-aloud time, just before *MND* rehearsals, I started reading it to the class.

It was as if Susan Cooper had written a book especially for our class. *King of Shadows* is the story of Nat Field, a 13-year-old actor. It's 1999, and Nat has just been chosen to play Puck in an all-boys version of *MND* to be performed at the newly-reconstructed Globe Theater in London. During the course of rehearsals, Nat is suddenly thrown backward in time, and ends up performing Puck in the original production of *MND*—in 1599—with William Shakespeare as Oberon.

The book is brilliant. Wonderful characterization, realistic historical detail, and an ingenious plot: Nat exchanges places in time with another boy actor, because the boy contracts bubonic plague and puts Shakespeare and the remainder of his career at risk.

The story was so perfectly relevant to what we were doing at that very moment, it was all I could do to limit the read-aloud period to one chapter a day. The kids loved it, and after we finished it, they each wrote a full-page letter to Susan Cooper, thanking her and explaining about our production. Many of them also wrote that we were raising money to go to OSF at the end of the year, to see Shakespeare live.

Pleased to get such an outpouring of writing, but expecting little to come of it, I copied the letters and mailed them off to Ms. Cooper, in care of her publisher, enclosing a note of explanation. Two weeks later, we got a handwritten letter from her, expressing her amazement at the coincidences and blessing our project. She also sent a check for $50.00 to add to our Ashland Fund. I framed the letter, and the signed photo she sent along with it, and put them up on the classroom wall. We were all thrilled, and felt we had been validated by One of The Famous. Susan Cooper knew how important it was to encourage kids, especially when they're trying something difficult; and one of the many nice undercurrents in *King of Shadows* is the strong support for Nat's troupe from their adult helpers and coaches.

For my purposes, this was so perfect. In the very first chapter of the novel, Nat is getting acquainted with the other actors, and they start doing a trust-building exercise. It's called "Willow in the Wind"—and it was one which our class had also just started doing. Talk about serendipity! *MND* was the goal that drove us, but trust-building was the scaffolding that supported the dream, gave it a solid framework, and sustained it through the inevitable ups and downs of doing theater.

> *The best thing about doing MND was everyone helping each other. When someone fell, there was always someone to catch them.*

Since last year, I have doubled my trust in the other 6th-graders, and gotten more trusting with the 5th-graders. In other classes, people are scared to hold someone's hand, and when they see what we do, they're in awe.

Well, at first no one knew me, so I felt left out. But now it just feels…right.

Boy do you trust everyone after this! I could be BLIND and still I would be able to perform on our stage!

I'm a lot closer to _____. We just seem to be able to talk to each other a lot better. One thing I really liked was that people in our class even helped those they weren't getting along with.

We're a lot nicer to each other, and we know each other better. And most of all we trust each other more.

If you do trust-building a lot, you do get really close.

I have made so many friends this year. Everyone is nice to everyone. I really think the saying, "Everyone does better when everyone does better" is true. I have a bigger variety of friends this year.

I've learned to trust others, and to be able to depend on them. Trusting them not to slap you too hard onstage, or when you jump on them not to let you fall. Depending on them not to forget to bring your costume, or when they do your make-up not to make you look like a freak, but make you feel exactly how you wanted.

"We are one big amoeba," L- said. Ha! So we are.

It didn't take too long for me to realize that if drama was going to work, if it was going to become the process that molded us into a functional group, processing circles would not be enough. We could talk and talk about problems, plans, ideas, feelings, conflicts, and "teamwork," but without some kind of hands-on model, lasting bonds among the students were not going to be forged. The circles were excellent for establishing the context. Our class ethic strongly supported inclusion, kindness, and empathy. For many kids, however, those were just words.

At the beginning of every year, each student in our class brought in a different set of experiences as a member of a large group. Some had been in our Options program for years, and were pretty much used to an inclusive model. New kids, on the other hand, usually came to us from more competitive situations, classrooms where academic and social hierarchies had been quickly established and were rarely challenged or upset. How to make this mix of experiences, backgrounds, and expectations a functional group? It seemed to me that if I could find a physical model—for building familiarity, connection, shared interest, and even trust—that they could learn and practice, it would be a big help to all of us.

Whatever I came up with, it couldn't just be theoretical, some kind of arbitrary behavioral ideal that was posted on the classroom wall and then ignored for the whole year. It had to actually work. It had to permeate the classroom, not just support theater. It had to show results—not just lip service to "respecting" others on the playground, but actual reaching out—kindness. Not just *quid pro quo* emotional barter (friendship deals, for example), but genuine inclusion.

The most common model for this at school was "teamwork," as in, everyone in class is a team player, working toward victory over… over…what? Something vague and meaningless. Or more often, working toward some extrinsic goal/prize/reward—an ice cream party, longer recess, etc.

I have so many problems with these concepts, and their assumptions, I hardly know where to begin—it's easily worth another book, but luckily, that book has already been written.* For one thing, no "team" as most of us understand the term is non-hierarchical. It's always apparent, to team members if not always to outside observers, who has high

---

* Alfie Kohn, *Punished by Rewards*. Houghton Mifflin, 1999.

status and who is lower on the tetherball pole. There are always different expectations for different rungs of the team ladder, and also different rewards. You must always have "respect" for teammates, but that almost never means including them in the activities of the favored. And so on.

The whole idea of motivating students with extrinsic rewards is another terrible but almost omnipresent part of social behavior at school. Fortunately, by the time I started doing drama, I never had to fight that battle in my classroom: it was one of the guiding principles of our wonderful Options Program that extrinsic rewards were detrimental to everything we stood for.

Instead of a team, I wanted our class to be a family. Our program itself aspired for students of all ages, teachers, and parents to function as an extended family, and at our best, that is what we were. The problem was size: with 80 - 100 students, acting familial was easier said than done. But with a smaller group, the 20 - 30 students I usually taught, it seemed possible to create a social structure that resembled a family. Of course brothers and sisters sometimes fought, and some families were dysfunctional. But the binding force was always there, a web of connections that offered something no team could match: kinship and interdependence.

The kinship part is fairly obvious—feeling that you are actually related to the other kids in your class by something more than age and grade. "Kin" is from the same root as "genesis"—suggesting our beginnings in our connected-ness. Of course the kids weren't related by blood (though we did have more than our share of siblings in the program). Even so, I hoped they could at least become a close-knit group of adoptees. Optimally, sharing a strong sense of solidarity, our rituals and traditions would make us into something Shakespearean, a *band of brothers* [and sisters]".

The "interdependence" part is more complicated. Even though it goes against the grain of our dominant culture, to admit dependence is only to be honest—especially for kids. To accept the dependence of others is also a cultural reach. But interdependence is different. It is the basic recognition that we need each other in order to thrive.

For my students to reach this level of bonding, they had to learn to trust each other. And the way to do that, I believed, was to play games.

It all started with informal hand-clapping games, which have long been popular in many urban schools. In 1993, during my K-8 teacher training, I interned for four months at Latona School in Seattle. An all-city-draw alternative school, Latona was home to students from 12 or 13 different ethnic groups. I saw many great things there, and one that stayed with me was the way students used hand-clapping games to connect with other students.

In 1999, I introduced some of this to my class, simple clapping patterns between two people. Very basic!

(1) Face your friend
(2) Clap hands, slap knees, clap hands
(3) Double slap with your friend
(4) repeat #2
(5) Single slap, right hands
(6) repeat #2
(7) Single slap, left hands
(8) repeat #2
(9) repeat #3, FASTER!

Like any kind of patterning activity, this was good for their brains, and for increasing coordination. The most important thing, for me, was how it helped them physically connect with each other. Naturally, every kid started the activity clapping with her friends. But I allowed only a few repetitions for each couple before clapping my own hands, and saying, "Switch partners!" The object was to get them to clap with kids they ordinarily had little contact with—kids outside their immediate friend-ship circle. Just the simple act of clapping with someone, I found, made each student more aware of the others.

From there, I moved on to the genre of alternative playground activities which, at that time, went by the rubric "new games." Back in the 70s, the New Games Foundation created a whole series of non-competitive games and activities to promote solidarity and trust-building. I had owned copies of their books for years—*New Games, More New Games*, etc.—but had never been motivated enough to try them out. Using these books, and the excellent similar titles by Karl Rohnke in the

Silver Bullets series, I started going out on the playground with my kids at recess, and at other times, to experiment with all kinds of different games.

New games are cooperative and interactive. Everyone gets to play, and very rarely is there a "winner." The stated object is simply to have fun, and of course what's really going on is that kids are learning to integrate themselves into a group activity in a way that makes it fun for everyone, not just the most coordinated.

"Human Knot" was a favorite: standing in a circle, people come together, grab hands with anyone except the people beside them, then back up and try to untie the knot without anyone breaking hands. Great for problem-solving, also great for basic human contact. And no group has ever played this game without laughing. A lot.

Even more fun was "Anti-Musical Chairs." Everyone who has ever played the original game as a child remembers the feeling of being put out—usually accompanied by laughter at your expense, for being too slow to find an empty chair when the music stopped. The new games version was specifically designed to eliminate those hard feelings. When the music starts, there is a chair for each person; when it stops, they all sit down. Then the music starts again—except now, while it is playing, the game leader removes a chair. This means that each time the music stops, all the kids have to find a way to sit on fewer chairs. This takes some real creativity. Kids can't plan who is going to be in their "chair group," so it's a good way for everyone to mix. And because of the physical contact, trust becomes more and more essential—it's hard to balance six people on a single classroom chair without lots of quick trust agreements. Kids loved this game, and the only problem with it is deciding when to stop—obviously, when you get down to three or four chairs, the risk of injury increases exponentially.

The list of possible cooperative games goes on forever. By trial and error, within a few years I found the 10 or 12 that worked best for us. To this collection I soon began to add the games that I was learning at various continuing education workshops I attended.

Around this time, Seattle Repertory Theater began offering a week-long summer workshop called "Bringing Theater into the Classroom." Seattle Rep staff, area actors, and local drama teachers gave classes on everything from readers theater to Shakespeare. The classes were excellent, and I also learned a lot from conversations with other teachers. Best of all, every class started with a series of warm-ups and trust exercises, many of which were very useful for my class.

Some of the activities we did were most appropriate as icebreakers. These were for the beginning of the year, to help kids get acquainted with each other, or for a newly-formed group, theater or otherwise. What we very un-originally called "The Name Game" is a very basic example. Starting in a seated circle, I would say, "My name is Bob, and this (pointing at the student to my left) is my friend John." Then John would say, "My name is John, and (pointing at me) this is my friend Bob." Then, the student next to John would say, "My name is Rebecca, and (pointing at John and me) these are my friends John and Bob." And so on, around the circle, with mounting excitement/anxiety about whether each person could accurately remember the names of everyone preceding him. New kids were not ridiculed, they were helped out by the class: it was entirely acceptable not to remember, and fun to try. Of course, I would always manage to sit between a new student and someone who—I was fairly sure—could name everyone in the circle. The value of this game was not simply in allowing each student to hear her name 20 or 30 times—which really helped us all remember the new kids—but also that loaded phrase, "my friends." The game assumes that all of us are already friends, with all the equality and solidarity which that implies.

Another good start-up was the "The Weaving Game"—especially effective on the first day of class. Students are seated in a tight circle on the floor; taking a skein of heavy yarn, I carefully unravelled 8–10 feet of it. Holding on to the free end, I named someone directly across the circle and carefully tossed the skein to him. He repeated the process, holding on to the strand of yarn and tossing the skein across the circle. The last person tossed the skein back to me, and what we ended up with was a spider web of yarn, stretched fairly tightly between all of us. At that point, I would produce an inflated balloon, 10–12 inches in diameter. Nothing needed to be said about what we would do with the balloon, it was obvious. I gently tossed the balloon out onto the yarn web. Working together, we tried to keep the balloon afloat on top of the web of yarn, without letting it slip between the strands. As a game, this is more difficult than it sounds—kids always tended to overreact, in their excitement, and invariably the balloon would fly out of the circle. We always started over, and eventually managed to be successful for quite a while. As a metaphor, on the other hand, it's extremely useful and simple: we are all connected, and for us to succeed at a common task, we must learn to work together. As after every game or activity, the processing discussion brought home the idea from the comments of the students themselves— the game is a perfect physical model of the idea of interdependence.

In addition to the games we played that centered on trust, we also tried more and more activities more accurately called drama games. In these, the focus is not so much on interdependence as on creativity, spontaneity, mindfulness, and cooperation. One we did many, many times was "What Are You Doing?" One player starts a motion—digging a hole, let's say. The person standing next to her in the circle asks, "What are you doing?" To which, the digger replies by naming any activity except what she's actually doing. "Oh, I'm brushing my hair with a chainsaw." Much laughter— because that's exactly what the questioner must now pantomime doing, brushing his hair with a chainsaw. (Obviously, the kids would always try to come up with something totally crazy for the next person in the circle to do.) The game continues around the circle, each successive student asking the question and attempting something weird, meanwhile thinking of something weirder for the next person to try.

There are hundreds of these games on the internet, and every teacher or leader will find the ones best for his group. I'll give one more example of a game that our kids loved: "This Is Not a Chair." For this game, I would find an ordinary object—a stapler, for instance, bring it into the circle, and announce, "This is not a stapler." Then I would ask the person next to me in the circle, "What is it?" The goal was to creatively use the stapler as something different—weed-eater, false teeth, cell phone, etc. (I added one rule to this game: whatever you turned the object into, it could not be a gun or a weapon—because I discovered early on how limiting to the imagination these choices are, and because I don't like guns.) The first time around the circle, this game goes fairly fast. And if you keep going, you find the creativity first sagging, then reviving and becoming more and more fantastic.

Mini-digression: this phenomenon was such a good lesson for me, and I had many productive discussions about it with my colleague Sue Dazey. Suppose you gave a two-year-old a brain-stretching toy, and he didn't have a clue what to do with it, but he played with it in his own way for a few minutes, and then ignored it. Instead of discarding it and feeling foolish, what if you brought it back a month or two later? We asked our kids to do so many challenging things in the way of problem-solving, both individually and in groups. We both noticed that if, after you did an activity like this, you tried it again after a certain period of time had elapsed, the kids would almost always get different and better results. Their thinking was more functional and more productive. Perhaps, having done it once, they were more relaxed, and it was easier to assimilate the concepts involved. Having done some mental accommodating the first time through, they found that the problem was now simpler to think about, and their analyses and responses were usually of better quality. For whatever reasons, it gave us a lot of new ideas to try. It led me to see the value of doing a play not just once, but several times—and the phenomenon of building on and extending previous work always held true.

The best drama games were those that *mixed* creativity, spontaneity, and interdependence. Kids had an opportunity to do something individually creative, within a framework that required adapting to group goals. A game they asked for constantly, and one of the most famous of its type, is called—no one knows why—"The Martha Game." All I had to do was say those magic words, and immediately two-thirds of the kids had their hands in the air, wanting to start the game. Sometimes I gave them a scenario: pointing to a student, I would say, "You're a tree in the middle of the park." The student jumped up onto the stage and dramatically posed as a tree. Now, even more hands were waving. I called a name. This student jumped up onto the stage and "froze" as something/someone in the park, hopefully related to the "tree" (but not necessarily or obviously), announcing what she was as she posed. She might be a butterfly, perched on the tree's branch/shoulder. She might be a little old lady carrying a violin case, walking through the park. If she wanted to be slightly obnoxious, she might be a dog, peeing on the tree…there's always someone, and all you have to say is, "Keep it appropriate, please." The next student either added to the existing scenario—"I collect butterflies," with an obviously large net threatening the butterfly—or started something totally new—"I'm a hobo, sleeping on the grass." Sometimes, the completed scene was simply a collection of disparate images. Other times, multiple sub-plots developed, involving everyone and everything in the park. After everyone was onstage, I would count to three; on three, everyone had five seconds to act out the next step in their lives, then that scenario ended.

The next step was "Human Machines," a more structured variant of "The Martha Game." A volunteer would go up and stand, sit, or lie down in the center of the stage and start making some kind of repeating motion with his arms, legs, head, or any combination. A second student would join him and connect, in some simple or arcane or mysterious way, to the machine part mimed by the starter. For example, the first student might simply stand sideways and make alternate pushing motions with his arms. The second student might either stand behind him and copy him, stand behind him and change the motion into another plane, stand in front and "receive" the motion and transform it somehow, or anything else she might think of. After everyone was onstage, I would stop the extended machine and ask it to try and start up in some kind of sequence—which was more or less possible, depending on the shape and orientation. The results of this game are inevitably quite unusual—it's like an instant, spontaneous art installation! Kids always seemed to know when the big machine was getting too close to something "real," and then someone would be sure to add something totally out of left field—and much more interesting.

The idea that some kind of "hive mind" might be developing was always real to the kids—"Human Machines" was by far the quietest game we ever played. It was almost as if they were listening for some kind of inner revelation. And in that vein, they always liked the game called "Psychic Numbers," too. In a silent, seated circle, eyes closed, the group tried to sequentially say the numbers from one to x (x being however many there were in the circle), with each student saying only one number, and no two people saying a number at the same time—in which case, you start over. We tried this at the beginning of the year, usually ending it pretty quickly in frustration. About halfway through the year, though, every group was able to do it in fewer than 10 tries. Kids discussed many strategies for success, and one was simply being willing to wait through a certain period of silence before saying "your" number. Another was "not having to be the first or last person"—i.e., finding your place in the sequence, not trying to be "the hero."

Finally, we come to the core trust games, which are aimed at establishing basic social comfort zones, and then safely putting these zones at risk. In "Human Sculpture," the kids work in revolving teams of two. No talking is allowed. Taking turns, first one is the sculptor and one is the clay, then they switch. As I count to ten slowly, they model their partners into whatever shape strikes their imagination—always keeping the partner's physical safety and comfort in mind. At ten, I have them all take a look around at the "gallery" they've created. Then partners switch, and we repeat; then I have them pick new partners, and repeat again. Again, the object is not to create some amazing end product—there are only a limited number of things you can mold another person into in 10-15 seconds. The idea is to accept someone you are just getting to know moving your arms, legs, and head around—and your doing the same to them. The cold objectivity of being the clay helps, but this is an activity you have to work up to. At first everyone wants to do this activity with just their friends, of course, so the other big idea is to mix the kids with as many others in the class as possible. And post-game processing is essential: what did it feel like being the clay, being the sculptor, what did you notice about planning vs. just doing it freely, etc.

"Willow in the Wind," the game Nat Field and his fellow actors are playing in the first chapter of *King of Shadows*, involves small groups of five or six students, standing in a close circle, one student at a time in the middle. Spotters around the circle, closely side by side and facing inward, hold their arms up, palms out, knees flexed. The middle person, with his hands crisscross on opposite shoulders, eyes closed, and keeping his body as straight as possible at all times, asks "Ready?" to make sure the spotters are focused on him. At their "Ready!" he very slowly allows his upper body to fall outward, keeping his feet flat on the floor. The spotters do not let him fall more than 5–10 degrees before receiving his weight on their palms, then slowly moving him back upright and then around the close circle of palms—like a willow tree bending in a gentle breeze. This game requires a definite amount of preliminary discussion, and demonstration by experienced students, as well as the usual thorough processing afterward. It's not for every group, only those who have reached a certain level of confidence in each other.

And for those groups, sometimes it's possible to move on to "trust falls," a common feature of many ropes courses. This is where 8–10 students make a flexible ladder with their interlocked arms, and one student at a time falls backward onto the "ladder"—after MANY precautions, warnings, and under close supervision of the leader. And again, this one is definitely for smaller, older, more experienced groups.

But the final and best trust exercise is for everyone, for it embodies all the best qualities of the other activities, and then adds empathy. Just as *MND* was our signature show, "Guardian Angel" was our signature trust-builder. It started and ended every trust circle, and even the kids who had done it a hundred times (and who moaned when I announced it) did it willingly. They knew how important to the smooth functioning of our group it was.

Starting from a standing circle, the leader calls on each person by name to close her eyes, fold her arms (as in "Willow" above), and walk across the circle and back a certain number of times—usually four or six. No talking is allowed. Once the game has started, the leader may call on one, two, or even three more people to start their journeys across the circle while the first person is still walking back and forth. Those on the outside of the circle are the Guardian Angels, completely focused on the walkers. It is their responsibility to ensure that no walkers collide. If they see that this is about to happen, they must silently (so as not to confuse the other walkers) step forward and hold onto and/or re-direct someone, to prevent it. If a walker is named to start and his absence creates a gap in the outer circle, someone else must slide over and fill it, so that no one will walk through the circle and into a wall, table, etc.

The progress of any group may easily be determined by watching how kids walk across the circle in Guardian Angel. Kids new to our program would, naturally, walk very slowly and often "cheated" (i.e., protected themselves) by squinting through their eyelids. As we did it more and more, you could see them gain confidence. In addition, the number of protecting angels always increases as you go on. By the time you get to dress rehearsals and performances, kids are very intense about making sure everyone is guarded. To see a group of students play this game well is to see a group who have learned to be responsible for each other in a physical way. It is a group who, you can be sure, will not allow the people with whom they are onstage to fall.

It was really cool to watch everybody work together onstage. When someone forgot their lines, someone else onstage would say the words, or cue them.

The best thing was everyone helping each other. When someone fell, there was always someone to catch them. That's what Options is all about.

I learned that when people work together, they can do everything!

It was a great group to be working with. Trust-building was very helpful in getting us to know each other. We were like a big family.

The trust-building helped a lot. It made us understand each other better, because we felt each other's emotions. At the beginning of the year I didn't really fit in, but I really feel like I belong here now. It made me feel like an important person.

This is the place where I belong and the people I belong with. I feel like if I have a problem or say something wrong these people will never turn on me. The thing that really helped me was drama and trust-building. It made a connection with these wonderful people, every single one is different, but we have a lot in common.

I trust people more now. I feel like I've known these people forever because I worked with them for 10 performances.

Everyone has made me feel great and very welcome. When I first came I felt like a new person no one would like. But I feel different now. Very different.

It has helped me to be me and to trust others. And you can just come up to your friends and hug them, and they won't say, "You are so weird!"

I learned that it doesn't matter if you're with a boy or a girl. At other schools boys and girls are more separated, but here it's not like that, especially onstage.

When I was little, I wanted all my friends to be the same — nice, caring, and talented. I didn't have many friends, and I always wondered why, until now. To get along with other kids you have to accept them for who they are.

As always, I got the friendship and dependency of my friends, whom I enjoy hanging out and acting with. And it is so cool how strong the trust of our group is. We can understand each other without saying a word.

Since we depend on each other, it demolishes cliques.

This really brought out the best in me, it seems. I never really thought that I could one day be an actress or someone onstage. Right before we did this play, I had to make a really hard choice in life, and once I chose, it was gone forever. Every night I would sit in my bed and stare at the wall and think of my decision, and literally cry myself to sleep. But every single time we showed up for rehearsal I grew stronger and better. I always laughed every time. I remember being so happy when I was around everyone. It seems this came through right on time!

The trust-building really paid off. This is the first time I have felt really comfortable among my fellow actors. Getting feedback on how you did is great, too.

Doing this play with all of these people has helped me to realize how much love and trust can be in other people. I had never taken the time to watch others and realize that they did what they did with the help of others.

We are a family now. Doing this has made me realize how much stuff people have that they need to let go of. I realize now that I am not the only one with problems. Other people need help too. It's helped me learn how to trust people.

I trust people a lot more and everyone, in a way, understands each other better after performing two plays together. It's like everyone is connected somehow.

Well, before the actual performances all of the trust-building was a little shaky, but during the performances we showed more trust in one performance than in three weeks of trust-building activities. My relationships are different now, I trust this class more than I ever have.

I have grown 101% closer to my classmates. I could probably list the favorite food of 3/4 of them. We are a close group.

In a way I can't explain, you look at them differently, you feel different, you are different. There's a connection, an unbreakable string.

I felt like the play was one big trust-building game. It made me get a lot of friends who encouraged me. I feel really tight with everyone. I feel like this is a second home, that I'm always looking forward to.

I've realized that friendship is a lot better than power. Because before I just thought if you had power then you had friends. But it's not really that way.

The play is a lot about trust, and if someone forgets or messes up a line, instead of yelling at you and saying you're stupid, here they just smile and joke later and they don't try to hurt your feelings.

We are more like a family than ever. Now no one is like, "I don't want to sit next to <u>them</u>." And also, people are mingling with people I would never think they would be with.

I think I get along better with people I didn't get along with before. I have gotten to be better friends with the boys in class. The play has nurtured many kids in this class, including myself. We have become a tight family, even more than last year. I think that is really big. I don't think that any other class could do that.

Building trust helps drama, and doing drama builds trust.

It has really taught me that I can trust people. It doesn't matter who they are. If I miss or skip a line I feel like they will fix it, or at least cover it up. And if you try something new or anything onstage, they will not make fun of that idea but support it. I feel like they are more my friends because we have all worked together to do this play. If one single person had not been in this class it would not have been the same.

In the beginning, I wasn't really as close with everybody as I am now. The trust-building has helped, and it's a lot more like a family now. In the beginning of the year people were kind of mean to each other, but not any more.

It has made me trust people more, and I feel closer to people now. I think before we started this play I was a little hesitant to really get to know everyone. But while we were doing it I started to talk and get to know everyone for who they really were, and I have more friends now.

Love and togetherness. We have that, and it is great.

I remember just hearing people mess up. And other people saving them.

It worked because this class has so much magic in it. We might not know it, but we do when we go onstage together. All of the pieces of the puzzle that might be lost find their way to the super glue!

I remember all the little pieces being put together to make the play happen. But most of all I will remember the friendship and trust, which worked as a glue to hold the pieces together.

At the start of one school year, knowing I would have 24 students in my class, I was lucky enough to find a high-quality jigsaw puzzle with only 24 pieces. On the first day, I gave each student a piece in an envelope, and after our opening circle, they all got together and completed the puzzle. A small thing, but several of them never forgot it. We've all had the frustrating experience of missing a puzzle piece, and many kids have had the experience of either not fitting in, or not finding a place for themselves. Trust-building proved to be a really good way of constantly reinforcing the idea that all the pieces were needed to see the whole picture. Two early entries in my sporadically-kept journal:

We were having a class meeting to talk about the cliques that we felt were developing. They were marginalizing several kids, and keeping us from doing the play. We went around a few times, everyone talking pretty honestly about how it made them feel. Except A-, of course—mute as usual. [A- was the most marginalized student, few friends] *Finally we got to a point where we had to decide what to do. After a long silence, J-* [most popular kid in class] *got up, walked over to A-, sat down by him, put his arm around him, and told him, publicly and sincerely, that he was sorry for the way they had all treated him, & offered friendship. Group dynamic changed completely!*

We were outside on the playground, trust-building. Six kids, all sizes, both genders, trying to figure out how to arrange themselves in a circle, holding wrists, so that they could all lean back and remain balanced—or at least not fall down! They kept making different circles. Leaning back, falling over. Laughing hysterically. Getting up, trying again.

Trust-building made a big difference in my life as a teacher. Knowing that almost every day we would not only have a processing circle, but also do some kind of drama game or trust activity, students were more willing to participate actively in group projects, and these became more equitable and more productive. Before, some kids were only agreeable to working with friends; now, they found it easier to work with anyone in class. For the drama project, it meant I was able to challenge them even more, and so I began to try plays outside our comfort zone *(MND)*. And that's when the really amazing things began to happen.

photo by Isabel Gates

Puck and the Fairies. [*A Midsummer Night's Dream*]

It Is a World to See

The first big step into the unknown that we took was *Much Ado About Nothing*. One of Shakespeare's so-called "dark comedies," in many ways *Much Ado* is at the other end of the comedy spectrum from *MND*. *MND* is fantastic and dream-like; *Much Ado* is generally considered Shakespeare's most realistic play. It's one thing for middle-school students to do *MND*—most of the characters are archetypal: the King and Queen (two sets), the angry father, betrayed lovers, pompous simpletons, mischievous spirits, etc. The characters in *Much Ado* are much more complicated, and the story has several strange twists. At several points in the play, even though we the audience know it's a comedy, we aren't at all sure it will have a happy ending.

There are two plots. One involves the "war of wits" between Benedick and Beatrice, and how their friends try to trick them into falling for each other. The other plot involves Benedick's best friend, Claudio (both are soldiers under Don Pedro), and Beatrice's cousin, Hero (daughter of Leonato, the governor of Messina). At the start of the play, they fall in love and become engaged. But jealous and vengeful Don John (Don Pedro's illegitimate brother) plots to ruin their marriage, with the help of his henchmen, Borachio and Conrad. They spread false rumors about Hero—that she is unfaithful to Claudio; Claudio believes the rumors, and renounces her at the altar. Hero faints, and is left for dead by Claudio, Don Pedro, and Don John.

Fortunately, the truth is discovered by the "brave" watchmen and constables of Messina, led by Dogberry and Verges. Borachio and

Conrad confess. Claudio repents to Leonato, who tells him to atone for the slander and apparent death of Hero by mourning at her tomb, then marrying her cousin—who turns out to be, of course, the original Hero herself. When Benedick and Beatrice are finally tricked into revealing their true feelings for each other, there's a happy ending after all, and a dance to celebrate it.

When they first saw the script (my version was about two-thirds of the original), many of my students were a bit intimidated. The plot was hard for them to keep straight, character relationships were confusing, there were many new words, and much more of the text was in prose, and thus harder to memorize. Being the veteran actors that they were, they read with an eye to staging, and they couldn't help but notice a few difficulties ahead. The set of *MND* was simple—Athens and the forest. The story of *Much Ado* moved from fancy ballrooms to a garden/orchard to small private rooms to a city alley at night to a beautiful chapel to a cemetery—how would we manage all that? Then there was the Big Dance in the first part of the play (which repeats at the end): not fairies twirling happily in the forest, but a formal Elizabethan dance, with four pairs of characters speaking and dancing at the same time. Yikes!

> *I remember at first memorizing without understanding what the lines meant.*

> *At first I didn't want to do it. I thought I'd never understand it.*

> *I had no idea how complicated it really was. Then I found out how deep the words were, and I got to find out what the words meant.*

> *My first impression of Much Ado was probably, "It's cool, but it doesn't make much sense!" I remember having to do the chapel scene so many times.*

> *I remember thinking Beatrice and Hero were the same person, and that the Watchmen got drunk, not Borachio and Conrad.*

At first I had no idea how anyone fit into the play, but later I found out. I remember during dress rehearsals all the Benedicks and Beatrices looked like hugging robots the first few times.

I didn't get it at all until dress rehearsal, then I got a chance to understand my characters.

I remember when I first found out we were doing Much Ado I didn't want to do it, because I remembered when my sister did it and I got sooo bored watching it, because I didn't understand it. Now that I was doing it I thought, how on earth am I going to memorize all that. But somehow I ended up understanding it and memorizing it.

The hardest part was first getting the script and trying to get a good understanding of what this play is about.

At first I couldn't understand the story, and I was sure I never would.

Fortunately, there was an outstanding BBC video of a famous made-for-TV Royal Shakespeare Company production from 1985. I still haven't seen a movie version of *MND* that I consider good enough (i.e., dark enough in the right way, not played for laughs) to use as a model. But the BBC version of *Much Ado* is brilliant, and we watched it several times—parents too.

Though so different from *MND* in so many ways, *Much Ado* does have a lot going for it, both in dramatic terms and as a challenge for young actors. A "dark comedy" in terms of plot twists, yes, but still definitely a comedy. The humor is of a totally different kind: it comes from witty insults, sharp sarcasm, and Dogberry's wonderful malapropisms and pompous ignorance. *Much Ado* has star-power—the main characters are very forceful and individualized. When you do finally get it, when you finally understand the lines and how to read between them a bit, many parts of it have a very contemporary feel—especially the Benedick—Beatrice skirmishes, and Benedick's direct stream-of-consciousness appeal to the audience:

> *They say the lady is fair; 'tis a truth, I can bear them witness.*
> *And virtuous; 'tis so, I cannot disprove it; and wise, but for*
> *loving me. By my troth, I will be horribly in love with her. I may*
> *chance have some odd quirks and remnants of wit broken on me,*
> *because I have railed so long against marriage: but doth not the*
> *appetite alter? A man loves the meat in his youth that he cannot*
> *endure in his age. No, the world must be peopled. When I said*
> *I would die a bachelor, I did not think I should live till I were*
> *married. Here comes Beatrice. By this day! She's a fair lady. I do*
> *spy some marks of love in her.*

How our Benedicks loved to blurt out that line—*"the world must be peopled"*—simply for the shock value. Everyone recognized that Benedick could be incredibly self-important. (After all, he would just be marrying her because the world needed more children.) And that was part of his charm.

But the big thing that *Much Ado* has going for it is that it has several of the most dramatic scenes that Shakespearean actors ever get to play, and that is why it is often called "the actors' play":

(1) The dance scene is one. The primary characters, masked, are exchanging partners and being witty. Beatrice, knowing that her masked partner is really Benedick, gets off some brilliant barbs, and he is helpless to answer. Hard to stage, but when we did it right it really charged them up.

(2) The two successive "gulling" scenes were very popular. In the first, Benedick's friends, pretending not to know he's listening, discuss how thoroughly Beatrice is in love with him. His reactions, visible to the audience, are wonderful to watch. In the next scene, Beatrice's friends do the same to her.

(3) Dogberry's bumbling arrest and "arraignment" of Borachio and Conrad, and his mixed-up recounting of it to Leonato, are the comic highlights of the play. The kids loved it.

DOGBERRY
> *You are thought here to be the most senseless and fit*
> *man for the constable of the watch; therefore bear you*
> *the lantern. This is your charge: you shall comprehend*
> *all vagrom men. You are to bid any man stand, in the*
> *prince's name.*

Second Watchman
> *How if he will not stand?*

DOGBERRY
> *Why, then, take no note of him, but let him go; and*
> *presently call the rest of the watch together and thank*
> *God you are rid of a knave.*

(4) The favorite scene by far—and the all-time best scene in all of Shakespeare for young actors (in my humble opinion) was the chapel scene. Almost everyone is in it, and it's very dramatic and moving. It begins with Hero and Claudio about to be married—but then Claudio accuses her of being unfaithful, and she faints. Huge uproar. Finally, Friar Francis comes up with a scheme to save the day. Everyone exits except Benedick and Beatrice, who is weeping for her cousin's shame. Beatrice's righteous anger on Hero's behalf causes Benedick to show the true colors of his nobility, and they confess their love for each other. Then, in a turnaround that is so typical and brilliant of Shakespeare, this:

BEATRICE
> *You have stayed me in a happy hour: I was about to*
> *protest I loved you.*

BENEDICK
> *And do it with all thy heart.*

BEATRICE
> *I love you with so much of my heart that none is left*
> *to protest.*

BENEDICK
> *Come, bid me do any thing for thee.*

BEATRICE
> *Kill Claudio.*

Claudio is his best friend, so Benedick has to choose between the two of them. The subsequent intensity of Beatrice's bitter anger, and his halting response, is so dramatic that it was always the ultimate drop-of-a-pin moment for everyone, cast and audience. This scene has it all—anticipation of joy—then shock and embarrassment—despair, anger, panic—then quiet devotion—then more shock!—then a perfect resolution. Lots of physical action—Hero collapses, her bridesmaids frantically try to revive her, her father head-bowed in despair, Beatrice kneeling, crying, trying to leave while Benedick pulls her back. This scene alone is worth all the effort it takes to do *Much Ado*.

The farther we got into the play, the more the kids realized that this was a play that depended very heavily on correctly understanding and speaking the words. As a result, we paid a lot of attention to pronunciation, meaning, expression, and gesture. It was intense. At first, even the better readers were stymied by some of the passages—such as this one:

> BENEDICK
>
> *O, my very visor began to assume life and scold with her.*
> *She told me, not thinking I had been myself, that I was*
> *the prince's jester, that I was duller than a great thaw,*
> *huddling jest upon jest with such impossible conveyance*
> *upon me that I stood like a man at a mark, with a whole*
> *army shooting at me. She speaks poniards, and every word*
> *stabs. I would not marry her, though she were endowed*
> *with all that Adam had left him before he transgressed.*
> *She would have made Hercules have turned spit, yea, and*
> *have cleft his club to make the fire, too. Come, talk not of*
> *her. I would to God some scholar would conjure her, for*
> *certainly, while she is here, a man may live as quiet in hell.*

Once we ran through this a couple dozen times, though, and in context, it began to make sense to them, as did the rest of the play. And it took me a month or so, the first time we did it, to realize that the kids were finding a better way to figure things out: through their characters. When I finally understood this, things went smoother, and I learned something important about how they came to terms with challenging material—not by close analysis, but by personalizing it. They wanted to understand Benedick and Beatrice—why were they so mean to each other, and yet so obviously drawn to each other at the same time? They loved how the villain, Don John, was so unashamed of his desire for revenge—where did it come from? (We had a long discussion about the notion of illegitimacy.) The romantic attachment of Hero and Claudio seemed simple enough to start with, then Claudio turns paranoid and ruins everything. How, the kids wondered, could he be so blind? How could Hero still love him? And so on. Dogberry and company provide wonderful comic relief—

> DOGBERRY
> *A good old man, sir; he will be talking: as they say, when the age is in, the wit is out: God help us! It is a world to see. Well said, in faith, neighbor Verges. Well, God's a good man; if two men ride of a horse, one must ride behind. An honest soul, in faith, sir; by my troth he is, as ever broke bread; but God is to be worshipped. All men are not alike; alas, good neighbor!*
>
> LEONATO
> *Indeed, neighbor, he comes too short of you.*

—and then, they become essential to the plot and the happy ending: the kids liked the irony of that. As usual with Shakespeare, the "supporting" characters took on more and more importance the closer we looked at them.

As the production began to come together, we started taking advantage of a drama game I had picked up at a workshop. Called "Hot-Seating," this involved placing a willing actor in front of the class, in her role, while the class questioned her and called her to account for the things she did and said. It was like a press conference, and it proved to be an excellent way for the class to deepen their knowledge of the play and speculate about some of the mysteries. For the spotlighted actor, it was even better: she got to talk about her life, her background, and her choices, and thereby extend her hold on the role.

If Hero were on the Hot Seat, for example, many students were interested in knowing how on earth she could forgive Claudio. Giving a good answer to this was hard, but it did give the actress playing Hero some good preparation for accepting Hero's mind-set at the end of the play.

Their struggles to understand and accept their characters were much on their minds when they responded to the whole *Much Ado* experience:

> *I felt a lot different playing Beatrice than I did playing Hermia. Beatrice seemed a more realistic role, she also seemed more like me than Hermia did.*

> *At first, you think Don John is okay, then he turns out to be the mastermind behind the slander of Hero. And Claudio, I remember Claudio saying his, "Oh Hero, what a hero hadst thou been" line with such disgust and contempt.*

> *I didn't want to be Hero. I remember thinking maybe there was a possible way of quitting and having someone else be Hero. I was so nervous about her scenes, especially the wedding scene. And guilty about not being memorized. But finally I did it, so I wouldn't let my friends down, or myself, or Hero.*

> *I remember thinking how stupid the part of Leonato was— and how awesome it turned out to be.*

> *I remember thinking how shameful it all was for Leonato, and how embarrassing for Hero.*

> *I felt sad as my character, because I was involved in a slanderous plot against Hero.*

> *I remember feeling really mad at Hero, actually feeling angry at L-, who was playing her, like she was my real daughter who had done that.*

I remember being confused about how to play my character, and also how to think of her: do I like her? do I hate her?

You get a lot of mood swings in a play. You have to deal with the character you have, make the best of it. Think positive. When you put yourself in your character's shoes, you act better and you aren't as nervous.

It totally surprised me [as Claudio] *when I started screaming at Hero, and actually being angry.*

In Much Ado we did things that I haven't seen done before, for instance doing it modern, with more freedom for the costume ideas. Getting the emotions right for the characters I had was harder in this play, also having to show several emotions in one scene.

Leonato wasn't fun to play, until I got into his shoes.

At first I thought that the characters I was playing were dull and uninteresting, but they tested my acting ability. It was a challenge, but when we internalized our characters it worked.

Benedick is NOT humble. He's the kind of person that manages to invite himself to your party.

Don Pedro seemed like the cool kid, he was The Prince, and the boss. Claudio was just a stubborn brat sometimes, and sometimes he seemed to show off. And Dogberry just cared about himself. Like it went from GOD to DOGBERRY to VERGES.

Conrad definitely had the wrong idea about being a gentleman.

Beatrice was ALIVE!

All the characters seemed different after I started to listen to what they were saying. Leonato was strict and scary at first, but he turned out to be just protective.

Leonato wasn't fun until I got mad.

In the end, Hero was very cool. I wanted to quit, but one of my friends said I should give it a try, that it would be a great memory. And it is.

To me, Benedick always seemed a smart, witty person, but that was all. Playing him helped me see that even very smart people can do stupid things, but that sometimes that's okay.

Hero was innocent, but she could be hurtful if she wanted to be.

Beatrice seemed a little boring at first, but then I started to understand the meaning of things better, and it became a lot more fun and exciting.

I remember not seeing the costumes but the characters, who seemed to feel, think, and see. I remember feeling as though I was complete, or somewhat small compared to the immense world of Messina, and the even more immense world of thought. I remember hearing lines, or something more even than lines, it was thought and discussion.

I remember my character taking over, and not knowing what I was saying.

The chapel scene was my favorite. Because a lot of things have happened in the last three years, and as Claudio I feel like I can be mad about it, and as Hero I can cry about it.

As they got more and more caught up in the play, the kids started thinking more about how we would stage it. For us, *MND* had been focused mostly on costumes. Few props were needed, and as previously mentioned, the set was fairly simple. *Much Ado* would require a lot more detail, we decided, to make the realism of the theme convincing. Fancier costumes (including a wedding dress and a veil), fancy masks for the big dance, pikes for the watchmen, letters for the messengers, quill and ink for the sexton, and many other props were needed. We used portable trellis panels for the garden scenes, and draped them with heavy curtain cloth for the wedding scene. We made a tomb for Hero out of two black boxes and some black cloth. For the night-time alley scenes, we built some free-standing flats, hung ropes on them, and littered wooden boxes around. It was all just realistic enough to help the actors—and hopefully the audience—suspend their disbelief. It was impressive to watch the students jump into these technical aspects of drama. We didn't have much to work with in the way of resources, but we became experts at making do. Instead of just worrying about their costumes, the kids started getting interested in working our (very basic) light system, managing the props, and shifting the set between scenes. Handwritten "run lists" began to appear taped up backstage—a good sign that they were getting serious.

It was probably to be expected that our performances of *Much Ado* would have more glitches than those of *MND*. We had some memorable mess-ups, verbal and physical. The experience of doing *Much Ado* was on a different plane—for most of them, it was their first time doing something more serious onstage. But processing circles, trust-building, and having *MND* under their belts all helped make it work out okay.

I remember mess-ups, and ways to fix them. I remember frantically memorizing Friar Francis 20 minutes before I went on, feeling sort of sick because I was so nervous and excited.

I was really tired and really excited. How amazed I was! Even with mistakes, we did it!

I remember falling with my mistakes and knowing and trusting others to catch me.

I still can't believe we did it. That amazing jumble of words and emotion. So much heart was put into it. I feel like I've traveled through time, and now I'm back in the present. I miss my travels already.

Lots of people working together. There was a lot of magic —like when M- knocked the flat over, someone caught it, and we still went on with the scene. We were covering for each other, and it was just magic.

MC- yelling, glaring, and sneering as Don John. H- as Leonato, yelling at Dogberry. K- slapping Don Pedro. The dark stage, with only the blue lights, being filled with mourners. T- and M- dancing, looking like and BEING Don Pedro and Hero.

I remember hearing crying in the audience, and the yells, murmurs, and speeches of people onstage. The thumping of props going onstage. The whispers of actors saying, "You're on next scene."

I felt really excited when I said my lines correctly. And afraid that I would mess up, but it didn't matter. And at our cast's night performance it was just the feeling of, YES!

That feeling of togetherness, you know you can't do anything without everybody and they can't do it without you. That if you mess up they'll help you. If you fall, they'll catch you. And it's one of the best feelings in the world, knowing that all these people care about you. That you care about them, too!

In the beginning, I thought the play would work and be okay. But in the middle it fell apart, and I thought it would never work. In the end it did work, and it was so great, and I thought,

"We won."

I loved it when D- took over for J- and said the "Dost thou not suspect my place" speech. Go D-!

D- as Verges doing the enormous Dogberry speech, catching J- when she didn't know it. That was so cool, because at the beginning of the year he would never have gotten that into it.

I remember the beginning, getting our parts. Then finishing memorizing, thinking that was the end, but it was really the beginning again. Then all the talk circles and beautiful speeches from the heart to prepare all of us for what lay ahead, and what lay ahead was a miracle.

The music of the dance, the smell of Hero's perfume, the sight of the dance and the whole play, the wonderful feeling of BEING my part.

K- as Dogberry, stooping down and staring me in the eye, after the line when I called her an ass.

Our class was a lot closer for Much Ado, and we did a lot better. I think we had better audiences for MND, it's an easier play to understand. Much Ado is confusing, and most audiences don't get it because there are so many plots, and the funny stuff is in the words, not the action.

A lot of people really stepped it up this year. Some I would never ever imagine! I am very proud of those people. And everyone else! I noticed that I started to fall in love with this play. What a fool I am!

The satisfaction of doing something difficult was substantial, and well-earned. We ended up performing *Much Ado* five times, every other year from 2001–2009. Every time we did it, it was a breakthrough experience.

Benedict. [*Much Ado About Nothing*]

The Alms-Basket of Words

The qualified success of our first production of *Much Ado* spawned a happy kind of Shakespeare madness. The sixth-graders who graduated out of my class made it plainly known that they wanted to do more, that they couldn't stand to stop doing something they enjoyed so much. Partly in response, and also to see what they could do after two years of performing Shakespeare, I started an after-school class called, simply enough, Shakespeare After School (SAS). And for my 5/6 class, I began to look at other plays that would challenge them a little more.

Over the next six years, we put together productions of five more Shakespeare plays. Besides continuing to do *MND* and *Much Ado* on a regular basis, my class did *Love's Labor's Lost, Macbeth,* and *As You Like It.* SAS, getting new blood every year from the kids coming out of my class, also did *As You Like It, The Winter's Tale* (twice), and *Hamlet* (twice). The more Shakespeare we did, the more of each original script I tried to add in. At both levels, the kids responded with enthusiasm.

In the next several chapters I want to describe briefly some of the attractions and problems of these new plays—Hamlet excepted, since it proved to be a special case, and I will come back to it. I also want to let the actors speak a bit more at length about each play: what was difficult, how they approached their new roles, and their thoughts and feelings about how the productions went.

What I saw happen during these years, in class and after school, was fairly unusual. Students were excited, and were willing to work hard and take some impressive risks. They endured rigorous practices, and often memorized hundreds of lines. In addition, they learned useful techniques, not only for drama, but also for making any kind of group work more productive—techniques which have served them well since graduating from our program. What is more, many of them made impressive intellectual gains in literacy, communication skills, problem-solving, and other academic areas. I saw some breathtaking leaps in creativity. And while I can't prove that they were emotionally healthier for doing this work, I firmly believe it.

When I first considered doing *Love's Labor's Lost (LLL)*, I knew almost nothing about it. An early-ish precursor of both *MND* and *Much Ado*, it is also very different. Like *MND*, it has a lot of big roles, and an amateur play production near the end. Like *Much Ado*, it has loads of sarcasm and wit, as well as a masked ball. One big advantage was that the lines were mostly poetry—I had noticed by then that Shakespeare's blank verse was much easier for kids to memorize than his prose. Also, many of the roles can be played by either boys or girls, and—as in *MND*—many of the roles are archetypal.

In contrast to *MND* and *Much Ado*, however, the ending is indefinite and even ambiguous. The four pairs of lovers, whose simultaneous courtships make up the heart of the plot, all seem just about to become engaged, and then comes news of a tragedy that makes a happy ending impossible. And even though the ending turns out to be more appropriate, dramatic, and…Shakespearean than any conventional wrap-up would be, it is still quite a jolt for the unprepared.

There are several intermingled comic plots. One involves a constable, a maiden of dubious virtue, and an endearing neer-do-well named Costard; another, a couple of pompous scholars; and a third, a self-important Spanish Don and his smart-aleck servant. The lovers have their comic scenes too, and one of the surprises of *LLL* is how several of these scenes involve takedowns of male pretension and arrogance by women characters. And related to this, one of the pointed messages of the strange ending is how much more thoughtful and mature the young women lovers are than their male counterparts.

The biggest drawback of doing *LLL* is the language. Although well-suited to the pretentiousness of the people Shakespeare was sending up, to modern ears it is truly a strange brew. If there had been an Elizabethan equivalent of the Monty Python troupe, this is what they might have sounded like. Two examples:

Light seeking light doth light of light beguile:
So, ere you find where light in darkness lies,
Your light grows dark by losing of your eyes.
Study me how to please the eye indeed
By fixing it upon a fairer eye,
Who dazzling so, that eye shall be his heed
And give him light that it was blinded by.

Most barbarous intimation! Yet a kind of insinuation, as it
were, in way, of explication; as it were, replication, or rather,
to show, as it were, his inclination, after his undressed,
unpolished, uneducated, unpruned, untrained, or rather,
unlettered, or ratherest, unconfirmed fashion.

This is satire, of course—against ivory-tower wits (#1) and above-themselves schoolmasters (#2). It's also a young playwright being self-indulgent (and showing off). *LLL* was an early comedy. That Shakespeare was trying to out-write and outwit his more educated competitors is one generally accepted theory about why some of the jokes are pushed so far. For my students and me, lines like these were intimidating at first. But I had access to several different versions of the *Complete Works*, and many of the footnotes to the text proved useful. Once again, I wrote marginal notes in their scripts to help them decode, and we also did many more pre-rehearsal read-throughs for this play, stopping frequently to talk about what the lines might mean and how to say them.

The other drawback is that the plot is filled with references to contemporary events—scandals, celebrities, and gossip from the late 1590s. The character of Don Armado was a parody version of an actual visitor to London from the Spanish court, infamous for his outsized ego, and the lovers were loosely based on well-known courtiers of the time. The original audiences for *LLL* would thus have appreciated the satire in a way that is lost to us, and sometimes, hearing the lines, you feel as if you're not quite getting the joke. It's simply impossible for a modern version to use those resonances, and that makes this a challenging story to tell.

To compensate, I cut out as much of the topical material as I could, making more edits than usual in our script. And I decided to set the play on a college campus in the 1930s: the lovers were students, the constable a campus cop, Don Armado a visiting professor, the scholars Holofernes and Nathaniel resident professors, and so on. This didn't help the audience as much as it did the actors—it made several of the play's themes more understandable.

In the same way as happened with *Much Ado*, however, the kids used their characters, and the interactions among them, as their favorite way of becoming invested in the play. After four months of struggle, most ended up really liking the play, and would have repeated it if given the chance.

> At first I thought the Princess was really boring, but as I started playing her, I liked her better and better. She can be really exciting.

> I had no idea how much fun Holofernes was going to be. I knew Costard would be fun, but I had no idea being pompous could be so much fun. It was actually the stage directions and blocking (rather than their lines) that showed me the characters' personalities.

> I gave it my all, and realized that the Princess is funny, nice, mean, caring, rude, and fun to be around—but at the same time, she's responsible.

> Boyet was a complete mystery to me, at first. But every time I said my lines it added more to my character, and to ME. Performing Mercade made me feel like he actually came alive, that the King of France WAS really dying. It made it ALL feel real.

> For the first month I hated Longaville and loved Costard. But by the time we got to performance I liked them both. "They have lived long on the alms-basket of words" changed

my perspective of Costard, he's not just a guy who breaks rules and hangs around girls. And performing Longaville made me understand how important he was, so I began to like him more, and understand why he did what he did.

Ferdinand was a little more in control than I thought. At first he seemed like one of those "everybody likes me" guys. Costard is called a clown, so I automatically wanted him, but he is more serious than I thought. Ferdinand's first passage gave me a sense of control over the stage. Starting the play made me feel like more than just an actor. The performances make a difference. When you get up there and do comedy, and then do something serious, you totally change.

Holofernes turned out to be a lot more insane than I thought. The "verbosity" speech improved my idea of him, and acting the part really helped. Another thing that helped was seeing my counterpart act onstage.

At first I thought Dumain was kind and joyful. As we read the play more I saw that he was kind of sarcastic and sassy, and not very serious. I think the line "It's Biron's writing, and here is his name" really changed my idea of him, also all my lines making fun of the Worthies. In the end, Dumain was a lot like me, so it was kind of fun.

I remember the last dress rehearsal for Brabant cast. I figured it all out. That day my characters all became a part of me, and found a home inside me. And I'll never forget how it felt when it clicked.

I'll never forget the circles after the performances, how people would get compliments and always light up and be so happy. The laughing from the audience.

I'll never forget this. It's a gift that can only be given once in your life. The stage is the only place that exists for me now, and this gift will live on and will be given again and again.

I remember Bob saying that when I was offstage I was a balloon without air, but when I went onstage the ballon filled up!

Looking back at my copy of the *LLL* script, I noticed that it was probably the most heavily marked-up of all—definitions, blocking changes, Shakespeare's multitude of stage directions. Since *LLL* represented some of the toughest textual challenges we ever had, I want to go into a little more detail at this point about script-cutting. What follows is Shakespeare's original text is on the left, and our acting script on the right. (I have underlined the omissions.)

FERDINAND
Let fame, that all hunt after in their lives,
Live register'd upon our brazen tombs
And then grace us in the disgrace of death;
When, spite of cormorant devouring Time,
The endeavor of this present breath may buy
That honour which shall bate his scythe's
keen edge
And make us heirs of all eternity.
Therefore, brave conquerors,—for so you are,
That war against your own affections
And the huge army of the world's desires,—
Our late edict shall strongly stand in force:
Navarre shall be the wonder of the world;
Our court shall be a little Academe,
Still and contemplative in living art.
You three, Biron, Dumain, and Longaville,
Have sworn for three years' term to live with me
My fellow-scholars, and to keep those statutes
That are recorded in this schedule here:
Your oaths are passed; and now subscribe
your names,
If you are armed to do as sworn to do,
Subscribe to your deep oaths, and keep it too.
LONGAVILLE

FERDINAND
Brave conquerors,—for so you are,
That war against your own affections
And the huge army of the world's desires,—
Our late edict shall strongly stand in force:
Navarre shall be the wonder of the world;
Our court shall be a little Academe.
You three, Biron, Dumain, and Longaville,
Have sworn for three years' term to live with me
My fellow-scholars, and to keep those statutes
That are recorded in this schedule here:
Your oaths are passed; and now subscribe
your names,
LONGAVILLE
I am resolved; 'tis but a three years' fast:
The mind shall banquet, though the body pine:
DUMAIN
My loving lord, Dumain is mortified:
To love, to wealth, to pomp, I pine and die;
With all these living in philosophy.
BIRON
Dear liege, I have already sworn
to live and study here three years.
But there are other strict observances;

I am resolved; 'tis but a three years' fast:
The mind shall banquet, though the body pine:
DUMAIN
My loving lord, Dumain is mortified:
The grosser manner of these world's delights
He throws upon the gross world's baser slaves:
To love, to wealth, to pomp, I pine and die;
With all these living in philosophy.
BIRON
I can but say their protestation over;
So much, dear liege, I have already sworn,
That is, to live and study here three years.
But there are other strict observances;
As, not to see a woman in that term,
Which I hope well is not enrolled there;
And one day in a week to touch no food
And but one meal on every day beside,
The which I hope is not enrolled there;
And then, to sleep but three hours in the night,
And not be seen to wink of all the day—
When I was wont to think no harm all night
And make a dark night too of half the day—
Which I hope well is not enrolled there:
O, these are barren tasks, too hard to keep,
Not to see ladies, study, fast, not sleep!
FERDINAND
Your oath is passed to pass away from these.
BIRON
Let me say no, my liege, an if you please:
I only swore to study with your grace
And stay here in your court for three years' space.
LONGAVILLE
You swore to that, Biron, and to the rest.
BIRON
By yea and nay, sir, then I swore in jest.
What is the end of study? let me know.
FERDINAND
Why, that to know, which else we should not know.
BIRON
Things hid and barred, you mean, from common sense?
FERDINAND

As, not to see a woman in that term,
Which I hope well is not enrolled there;
And one day in a week to touch no food
And but one meal on every day beside,
The which I hope is not enrolled there;
And then, to sleep but three hours in the night,
And not be seen to wink of all the day--
Which I hope well is not enrolled there:
O, these are barren tasks, too hard to keep,
Not to see ladies, study, fast, not sleep!
FERDINAND
Your oath is passed to pass away from these.
BIRON
Let me say no, my liege, an if you please:
I only swore to study with your grace
And stay here in your court for three years' space.
LONGAVILLE
You swore to that, Biron, and to the rest.
BIRON
By yea and nay, sir, then I swore in jest.
What is the end of study? let me know.
FERDINAND
Why, that to know, which else we should not know.
BIRON
Things hid and barred, you mean, from common
sense?
FERDINAND
Ay, that is study's godlike recompense.
BIRON
Come on, then; I will swear to study so,
To know the thing I am forbid to know:
As thus,—to study where I well may dine,
When I to feast expressly am forbid;
Or study where to meet some mistress fine,
When mistresses from common sense are hid;
Light seeking light doth light of light beguile:
So, ere you find where light in darkness lies,
Your light grows dark by losing of your eyes.
Study me how to please the eye indeed
By fixing it upon a fairer eye,
Who dazzling so, that eye shall be his heed
And give him light that it was blinded by.

Ay, that is study's godlike recompense.
BIRON
Come on, then; I will swear to study so,
To know the thing I am forbid to know:
As thus,—to study where I well may dine,
When I to feast expressly am forbid;
Or study where to meet some mistress fine,
When mistresses from common sense are hid;
Or, having sworn too hard a keeping oath,
Study to break it and not break my troth.
If study's gain be thus and this be so,
Study knows that which yet it doth not know:
Swear me to this, and I will ne'er say no.
FERDINAND
These be the stops that hinder study quite
And train our intellects to vain delight.
BIRON
Why, all delights are vain; but that most vain,
Which with pain purchased doth inherit pain:
As, painfully to pore upon a book
To seek the light of truth; while truth the while
Doth falsely blind the eyesight of his look:
Light seeking light doth light of light beguile:
So, ere you find where light in darkness lies,
Your light grows dark by losing of your eyes.
Study me how to please the eye indeed
By fixing it upon a fairer eye,
Who dazzling so, that eye shall be his heed
And give him light that it was blinded by.
Study is like the heaven's glorious sun
That will not be deep-search'd with saucy looks:
Small have continual plodders ever won
Save base authority from others' books
These earthly godfathers of heaven's lights
That give a name to every fixed star
Have no more profit of their shining nights
Than those that walk and wot not what they are.
Too much to know is to know nought but fame;
And every godfather can give a name.
FERDINAND
How well he's read, to reason against reading!
DUMAIN

FERDINAND
How well he's read, to reason against reading!
DUMAIN
Proceeded well, to stop all good proceeding!
LONGAVILLE
He weeds the corn and still lets grow the weeding.
BIRON
The spring is near when green geese are
a-breeding.
DUMAIN
How follows that?
BIRON
Fit in his place and time.
DUMAIN
In reason nothing.
BIRON
Something then in rhyme.
FERDINAND
Biron is like an envious sneaping frost,
That bites the first-born infants of the spring.
BIRON
Well, say I am; why should proud summer boast
Before the birds have any cause to sing?
At Christmas I no more desire a rose
Than wish a snow in May's new-fangled mirth;
But like of each thing that in season grows.
FERDINAND
Well, sit you out: go home, Biron: adieu.
BIRON
No, my good lord; I have sworn to stay with you:
Give me the paper; let me read the same;
And to the strictest decrees I'll write my name.
FERDINAND
How well this yielding rescues thee from shame!
BIRON
[Reads] 'Item, That no woman shall come within
a mile of my court:' Hath this been proclaimed?
LONGAVILLE
Four days ago.

Proceeded well, to stop all good proceeding!

LONGAVILLE
He weeds the corn and still lets grow the weeding.

BIRON
The spring is near when green geese are a-breeding.

DUMAIN
How follows that?

BIRON
Fit in his place and time.

DUMAIN
In reason nothing.

BIRON
Something then in rhyme.

FERDINAND
Biron is like an envious sneaping frost,
That bites the first-born infants of the spring.

BIRON
Well, say I am; why should proud summer boast
Before the birds have any cause to sing?
Why should I joy in any abortive birth?
At Christmas I no more desire a rose
Than wish a snow in May's new-fangled mirth;
But like of each thing that in season grows.
So you, to study now it is too late,
Climb o'er the house to unlock the little gate.

FERDINAND
Well, sit you out: go home, Biron: adieu.

BIRON
No, my good lord; I have sworn to stay with you:
And though I have for barbarism spoke more
Than for that angel knowledge you can say,
Yet confident I'll keep what I have swore
And bide the penance of each three years' day.
Give me the paper; let me read the same;
And to the strict'st decrees I'll write my name.

FERDINAND
How well this yielding rescues thee from shame!

BIRON
Let's see the penalty. 'On pain of losing her tongue.'
Who devised this penalty?

LONGAVILLE

DUMAIN
This article, my liege, yourself must break;

Marry, that did I.
BIRON
Sweet lord, and why?
LONGAVILLE
To fright them hence with that dread penalty.
BIRON
A dangerous law against gentility!Reads
'Item, If any man be seen to talk with a woman
within the term of three years, he shall endure such
public shame as the rest of the court can possibly devise.'
This article, my liege, yourself must break;

Like Al Cullum, I always hoped to retain Shakespeare's language and rhythm as much as possible, while making the play easier for my students to understand and to perform. (And actually, I never exchanged a modern word for one of his unless I felt that it was both too important and too obscure. In the ten different plays we did, I changed perhaps twenty words.) In this scene, Shakespeare's virtuoso flights of metaphor and artificiality are meant to give us a sense of how far removed from reality these four ivory-towered courtiers really are. Omitting some of their overblown rhetoric risks diminishing this. On the other hand, much of what they say is redundant, and making sense of it is difficult. There were audience pressures—after all, most of our performances were for school groups—and there was time pressure: we had an upper limit of two hours for our shows, and by the time I cut this particular script, I had a good idea of how many pages the final script should have. As a result, I was constantly hoping to strike a balance between keeping Shakespeare's magic and making it as accessible as possible to cast and audience.

The more of Shakespeare I read, and the more we did, the harder it was to cut. Biron's amazing paradox-choked riff about the superiority of a real life over losing oneself in books (it begins with *"Why, all delights are vain"*) is justly famous, and may have been one of Shakespeare's early challenges to critics who thought him under-educated. The truth of books, he seems to say, is too intense to be practically useful—and its intensity can blind us, like looking into the sun too long. How much better the light from a beautiful woman's eye—"dazzling" suggests a star, or jewel—that draws us to it with its charm. At the time, I believed the subtlety of this was probably beyond my students, and so I reluctantly cut it—also, of course, trying to make this first scene flow more smoothly. Now, thinking back on the later triumphs of the kids who played Biron, I wish I'd tried it, at least for the parent night shows, when we had more time available.

Very rarely, but sometimes, I gave lines to a different character than in the original—as in the last lines above, where I gave Biron's lines to Dumain. Biron has many times more lines than Dumain and Longaville combined, and I was hoping to spread the wealth a bit—and this speech didn't seem to be one that especially characterized Biron.

When Shakespeare After School (or its later incarnation, Changeling) did a play, I involved the actors more in script edits. As older students, with greater experience, they were more capable of helping decide what we should omit. And also, most of their shows were at night, with more time available. How this worked out in practice, however, was interesting. Inevitably, they would decide to restore more and more of their *own* character's lines. In some cases, I thought this prevented the dramatic tension from building as I hoped it would. We nearly had some classic actor-director clashes —but fortunately, with all the trust-building we did, it always got settled amicably. That magical phrase, "It's not about you, it's about us," coming from a long-time friend, seemed to work wonders.

Obviously, editing one of Shakespeare's texts involves a lot of personal preferences and difficult choices. I strongly favor ending up with a version that keeps as much of the plot-moving or character-developing dialogue as possible; that retains Shakespeare's own words and rhythms of speech and phrase; that conserves role equity as far as possible (by not omitting "minor" characters, by balancing line counts, etc.); and that facilitates both the dramatic tension and the performability of the story. Many different versions of all the plays we did were/are available commercially—"Sixty-Minute" versions and the like—and I was always hoping to find one I liked, to save the time of doing the cutting myself. Unfortunately, I never found one I agreed with. It seemed presumptuous enough to be cutting at all, and if you were going to do it, you better do it as respectfully as possible. The advantage was that I became much more involved with the play than if I had simply accepted someone else's version.

In terms of the sheer number of exhausting hours spent rehearsing, this play was probably the hardest of all—and we performed it 12 times. At some point I remember wondering if Al Cullum would approve, or think I'd gone over the edge…but then, afterward, reading the survey responses, the outcome validated all the work.

> *It was really fun. The last rehearsal is always the best, because I'd worked up to it, and it made me think, wow, am I ready for this? And, well, I was, I really really was!*

They were indeed ready. The performances were well received, the complicated story was told and understood, and the labor of love was not lost after all, but paid rich rewards.

> *It taught me trust, gave me confidence, voice projection, new ways to solve problems, new words, better memorizing. Better rehearsing. I learned how to change, how to be more engaged, listen better. New ways to do things onstage, and thinking outside the box.*

> *It has helped me learn to trust people much better. It has improved my vocabulary. Also I feel I can be more focused, and I have more patience with my work.*

> *It helped me control my anger. Also, if I was feeling sad, I could take my feelings out onstage, not on people. I trust people more, and if I have to do something I just do it.*

> *The way Jacquenetta and Costard played off each other! So many mixed feelings, seeing the audience's faces, hearing them laugh, the stage lights shining on my face. Everybody crying and hugging each other after the last performance.*

Light Thickens

In the last scene of *LLL*, there is another play-within-a-play (as in *MND*). Don Armado, Costard, the schoolmasters, and others are performing a pompous tableau to honor the four couples—who are responding with sharp, and sometimes cruel, mimicry and derision. Suddenly, a messenger enters, a servant of one of the visiting young women. Everyone senses bad news—almost as if they knew their ridicule would come back on them. In the sudden silence, the messenger announces that the young woman's father has died, and instead of celebrating their engagements to the four men, she and her three friends must return home immediately. Unlike in any other Shakespearean comedy, there is no wedding, only a kind of conditional postponement that depends heavily on the male lovers changing their behavior.

It isn't exactly tragic, but it isn't traditional comedy, either—it's Shakespeare. And it prepared the students a little for our next project. After seeing them rise to the challenge of *LLL*, I knew in my heart that my class was ready to try a real full-length tragedy.

The first year of theater, we had done a drastically abridged version of *Hamlet*. Although that production turned out well, afterwards I decided that *Hamlet* was more suited to the older kids, and focused on comedy for my class. After *LLL*, however, I knew that they needed a new challenge. What to do? *Julius Caesar* was out, simply because of the lack of roles for girls. *Romeo and Juliet* was a common choice, but was practically a cliche—I hadn't yet seen the OSF production that would change my thinking. *Othello, King Lear,* and *Antony and Cleopatra* were way beyond us. That left *Macbeth*.

I liked the play, and I knew the kids would get caught up in it. My big problem with it was, how would we stage the fighting? Our stage was just not big enough to handle that kind of swordplay. No matter how well we blocked it out, someone was sure to get hurt.

In the summer of 2002, we saw a memorable OSF production in the round at the New Theater. Valmont Thomas was brilliant in the lead role, but what made this version so different—and so perfect for me to see—was, no swords. Instead, they played all the scenes around a circular pool of blood—probably eight feet in diameter, right in the center of the floor (there was tiered seating, no stage). For the fighting, the actors—all wearing white tunics—circled each other around the blood pool, then slashed at each other with blood-smeared hands. The effect was stunning—especially a *coup de grace*, one long swipe across the victim's neck. As the play went on, more and more blood spilled onto the floor, and the actors' boots began to make sticking sounds as they walked or ran across it—adding to the horror. Their unchanged costumes carried the marks of battle for the remainder of the play, also a nice touch.

Finding effective staging solutions is an extremely important part of doing *Macbeth*. Since the murder scene and Lady Macbeth's sleep-walk scene are both late at night, lighting is a big issue—and the witches' scenes had to be dark too, of course. The battles, the castle, and the big banquet scene (at which Banquo's ghost appears) all needed some kind of specific look and distinctiveness. More problematic was the important scene at the end that takes place in England, where Malcolm is in exile. We were past the point where we could get away with simply putting up a sign on the stage that said "England"—but how could we make it work?

I had been reluctant to get too involved with technical matters. But besides the needs of this play, several things were pushing me in new directions. One was the way the kids had responded to previous plays. If they could do more and more sophisticated versions of *MND*; if they could do *Much Ado About Nothing* and *Love's Labor's Lost*; if the older kids could do a much bigger version of *Hamlet*—maybe they deserved to move beyond a couple of light stands and a patched-together curtain. Another factor was the brilliant parent couple who had begun to help me with (and educate me about) tech stuff. Paul was a lawyer, but before doing that he had a long and illustrious career as a stagehand and theater electrician in Seattle. Paul could do anything—lights, wiring, paint, build flats, and take apart ceilings (that got us in trouble, but not for a while). His wife, Patsy, was a gifted prop- and costume-maker. For these two, my worries about staging problems were laughable; they always had a solution, even for problems I didn't know we would have. Paul was always on call to fix lighting problems, and Patsy eventually moved into our green room, with sewing machine and ironing board. Howard was Patsy's creation, and when he proved too big for several of the taller kids who played Bottom, she made Howard II, a smaller and lighter—but just as wonderful—version. With these two guardian angels at my side, I began to think outside my shabby little cardboard box. And as our set and costumes and props became more functional and elaborate, the kids got more and more excited and engaged and creative about staging possibilities.

Unlike editing the scripts, staging was always a cooperative project. From the very beginning, the hottest topic of our processing circles was always, "What if we —- ." What if, when Puck appears in the middle of the workers' rehearsal, he changes all their costumes a little? What if Flute, as Thisby, comes out wearing high heels? What if D- does Time's long speech holding an hourglass (before the second half of *Winter's Tale*)? What if Helena is a nearsighted librarian—carrying a couple of encyclopedias—who trips as she enters? What if Hamlet starts eating the pages he rips out of the book? What if three people sang Balthasar's song together, in *Much Ado*?

Kids loved this! Whether they were personally involved or not, almost everyone in our class had an idea about how to do a scene, play a character, say a line. Sorting through these ideas and figuring out which ones would work—and discarding the rest without hurting someone's feelings—took up a lot of our circle time. Unlike most of the other brainstorming activities we did, this one actually dealt with something they could see and feel. Staging problems were the best kind to solve together: not only were they real problems that affected all of us, they almost never had one fixed solution. No matter how good an idea someone thought of, there was always the possibility that someone else might think of an even better idea—in the circle, onstage in rehearsal, or even in performance. Better yet, this kept everyone involved in the play, even those with smaller roles. You might not have that many lines to say, but if you found the perfect way to choreograph the mourners' procession in *Much Ado*, everyone would love it.

These discussions had the added benefit of reinforcing one of our cardinal rules for circle and stage behavior: always say yes. After always making sure that everyone knew there were life situations when you always said no, every so often we played a drama game called, "Yes, let's!" This was simple, very one-dimensional, and brainless—but since it was aimed at eliminating something that was potentially dangerous to our effectiveness, sometimes we had to do it. In a standing circle, someone starts with any kind of impossible scenario, and presents it to the person next to her: "Let's ride our bikes to Hawaii!" The next person, instead of saying something like, "No—that's impossible," has to say "Yes, let's, and then let's—." As in, "Yes, let's, and then let's mount them on surfboards and go bike-surfing!" The idea is not so much to think of something brilliant to add on, but to keep yourself from saying no. Because onstage, saying no is deadly! In rehearsal, beginning actors, getting fed a messed-up line, would sometimes say, "Wait, no, that's not right," or something similar. Which is, of course, the worst thing that can happen—much worse than saying the wrong line. "Yes, let's!" and processing circles reinforced the idea of always saying yes in some way—by ignoring the mistake, or by fixing it.

Some of the most talented kids to come to our program were perfectionists in some way—either hard on themselves, critical of others, or both. Showing them the creative power of mistakes was one of the best things we gave them. You never hope that something goes wrong onstage, of course, but so many times, in so many shows, it was the glitches that got fixed creatively that everyone remembered best. What does a cast do, when all of a sudden someone skips ahead and omits a whole page of the script? Do you ignore it, and hope for the best? Sometimes. But what if something really important has been lost—a key to the plot, perhaps? What if someone's Big Moment—Titania's "forgeries of jealousy" lines, for example—has been lost? In that case, you do what I saw so many kids do on our stage: you go back, you re-cue someone to a pre-skipped passage, you conflate lines and patch something together—or you do some combination of all these things. You figure out how to make it work—not by taking a time-out from the ongoing action, by the way, but *while you are continuing the rest of the scene.* This happened over and over. When something went wrong, and everyone backstage knew it, we held our collective breath: what would happen? You could practically see the smoke coming out of their ears onstage, they were thinking so hard about possible solutions. Finally, if the omission was too important, someone would step up and take a chance.

I saw this happen numerous times in the catfight scene of *MND.* This is a tough scene in many ways—so active, so many lines for all four characters and so many of them very similar—and it rarely went off perfectly. And most of the time, it was okay anyway. But sometimes, if certain key lines were left out, it looked like the girls might never get to actually fight—disaster! When that happened, I saw many creative solutions: Puck (who is invisibly onstage for the scene) might whisper a good re-start line to someone; Lysander and Demetrius might distract the audience by scuffling, while the two girls quickly whispered ideas to each other; and so on. We may have missed some lines, but we never missed the actual combat—everyone knew we had practiced that way too much to simply let it go.

Besides saying yes, there are other important basics of staging a play that I should mention here. Saying the lines effectively came first—pronunciation, phrasing, and—especially with Shakespeare—rhythm. Pronunciation seems transparently simple, but with Shakespeare it was sometimes counter-intuitive, either because of the rhythm or because of Elizabethan differences. When Lysander proposes to Hermia that they elope, he says

> *A good persuasion: therefore, hear me, Hermia.*
> *I have a widow aunt, a dowager*
> *Of great revenue, and she hath no child:*
> *From Athens is her house remote seven leagues;*
> *And she respects me as her only son.*
> *There, gentle Hermia, may I marry thee;*

The word "revenue" is stressed on the second syllable, re-VEN-ue, rather than our REV-en-ue. I used to believe this was simply to serve the iambic meter (*of GREAT re VEN ue AND she HATH no CHILD*), but as it turns out, that's the way they said it. Similarly, in Helena's catfight accusation of the other three lovers —

> *Ay, do, persevere, counterfeit sad looks,*
> *Make mouths upon me when I turn my back;*
> *Wink each at other; hold the sweet jest up:*
> *This sport, well carried, shall be chronicled.*

the word "persevere" is spoken per-SEV-ere. If a word is pronounced "correctly' (i.e., the modern way) and it throws off the rhythm of the line, chances are pretty good that Shakespeare pronounced it another way.

Phrasing is important in all speech, but especially in a play, where it is essential to the expression of meaning and emotion. If you're trying to get an actor to speak a prose passage effectively in phrases, sometimes it helps to turn it into lines of poetry. Here's a selection from a contemporary play about the 1930s that we did twice, *Hard Times* (more on this play later). John the Red, a hobo, is talking to some friends about where his name came from.

> *Where I come from, anybody who causes trouble on the*
> *job, or who writes letters to the newspaper, or who thinks*
> *for himself at all, is called a Red. I ain't a member of that*
> *party, or any organized party. But I do hold with some of*
> *the things they believe, because I sorted em out myself and*
> *came to some of the same conclusions. And the trouble*
> *starts because I have a real hard time keepin my mouth shut*
> *when I see people gettin walked on, and not being able to do*
> *anything about it. I was in the Ford strike up in Michigan.*
> *We shut down the factory, & then the bosses called in the*
> *Guard, and then all hell broke loose. Well, I ain't no saint,*
> *I fought alongside my buddies. We used lead pipes, monkey*
> *wrenches, whatever we had. I guess, yeah, if we'd had guns*

we probably woulda used them too. But it wasn't a fair fight,
cause the Guard DID have guns and they used em on us. And
I didn't stick around after the fight, cause I knew they'd be
lookin for me. So here I am. Like you said, running from some-
thing bad to something better.

I had better luck getting the kids who played John to say this passage expressively when I gave it to them as a poem.

Where I come from,
anybody who causes trouble on the job,
or who writes letters to the newspaper,
or who thinks for himself at all,
is called a Red.
I ain't a member of that party,
or any organized party.
But I do hold with some of the things they believe,
because I sorted em out myself
and came to some of the same conclusions.
And the trouble starts
because I have a real hard time
keepin my mouth shut
when I see people gettin walked on,
and not being able to do anything about it.
I was in the Ford strike up in Michigan.
We shut down the factory,
& then the bosses called in the Guard,
and then all hell broke loose.
Well, I ain't no saint,
I fought alongside my buddies.
We used lead pipes, monkey wrenches, whatever we had.
I guess, yeah, if we'd had guns
we probably woulda used them too.
But it wasn't a fair fight,
cause the Guard DID have guns
and they used em on us.

And I didn't stick around after the fight,
cause I knew they'd be lookin for me.
So here I am.
Like you said, running from something bad
to something better.

Like music, almost any piece of prose has its phrases. For many younger actors, these are often hard to identify, and they tend to simply speak the lines until they run out of breath—sometimes without even pausing for punctuation. Lines of poetry are often easier for them to deal with than long speeches in prose, since they naturally tend to pause at the end of a line.

With Shakespeare's verse, the challenges are different. Since it looks like poetry, many students want to stop completely at the end of every line, regardless of the punctuation. This is almost guaranteed to make an audience lose the sense of what is being said. The correct way to read Shakespeare's verse is to read from punctuation to punctuation, with a very slight pause at the end of each line. Here is Macbeth, beginning to be gnawed with fear and doubt about what he has done.

We have scotched the snake, not killed it:
She'll close and be herself, whilst our poor malice
Remains in danger of her former tooth.
But let the frame of things disjoint, both the worlds suffer,
Ere we will eat our meal in fear and sleep
In the affliction of these terrible dreams
That shake us nightly: better be with the dead,
Whom we, to gain our peace, have sent to peace,
Than on the torture of the mind to lie
In restless ecstasy. Duncan is in his grave;
After life's fitful fever he sleeps well;
Treason has done his worst: nor steel, nor poison,
Malice domestic, foreign levy, nothing,
Can touch him further.

Here's the same passage, with slash marks inserted to show possible phrasing:

We have scotched the snake, not killed it:/
She'll close and be herself,/ whilst our poor malice
Remains in danger of her former tooth./
But let the frame of things disjoint,/both the worlds suffer,/
Ere we will eat our meal in fear/ and sleep
In the affliction of these terrible dreams
That shake us nightly:/ better be with the dead,/
Whom we, to gain our peace, have sent to peace,/
Than on the torture of the mind to lie
In restless ecstasy./ Duncan is in his grave;/
After life's fitful fever he sleeps well;/
Treason has done his worst:/ nor steel, nor poison,
Malice domestic, foreign levy, nothing,/
Can touch him further.

The purpose of this, of course, is to facilitate the sense of what Macbeth is saying. It has the additional advantage of making the passage substantially easier to memorize—and to say onstage.

Shakespeare was a poet before he was a playwright, and even his prose has built-in phrases. As with the verse, recognizing the phrasing helps audience and actor alike—with understanding and with expression. Here's Benedick, pondering the changes that falling in love has made in his friend Claudio.

I do much wonder that one man, seeing how much
another man is a fool when he dedicates his
behaviors to love, will, after he hath laughed at
such shallow follies in others, become the argument
of his own scorn by falling in love: and such a man
is Claudio. I have known when there was no music
with him but the drum and the fife; and now had he
rather hear the tabour and the pipe: I have known
when he would have walked ten mile a-foot to see a
good armor; and now will he lie ten nights awake,
carving the fashion of a new doublet. He was wont to
speak plain and to the purpose, like an honest man

and a soldier; and now is he turned orthography; his
words are a very fantastical banquet, just so many
strange dishes.

Using Shakespeare's punctuation to speak these lines is difficult enough for an experienced actor; for a young person, it's quite a challenge. Indicating phrases with slash marks makes it much smoother.

I do much wonder that one man,/ seeing how much
another man is a fool when he dedicates his
behaviors to love,/ will, after he hath laughed at
such shallow follies in others,/ become the argument
of his own scorn by falling in love:/ and such a man
is Claudio./ I have known when there was no music
with him but the drum and the fife;/ and now had he
rather hear the tabour and the pipe:/ I have known
when he would have walked ten mile a-foot to see a
good armor;/ and now will he lie ten nights awake,/
carving the fashion of a new doublet./ He was wont to
speak plain and to the purpose,/ like an honest man
and a soldier;/ and now is he turned orthography;/ his
words are a very fantastical banquet,/ just so many
strange dishes.

Just as recognizing musical phrases helps any musician, learning to see and hear phrases in prose or poetry is an essential skill for actors. When good phrasing is combined with finding the right *rhythm* of a passage, expression becomes even easier. In the very first lines of *MND*, Theseus is announcing—to Hippolyta and to the audience—coming events and the tone in which we will hear and see them:

Now, fair Hippolyta, our nuptial hour
Draws on apace; four happy days bring in
Another moon: but, O, methinks, how slow
This old moon wanes!

How is an actor to say this passage? There are many interpretations, but Shakespeare gives us several clues in the rhythm and phrasing (underlined words and syllables are stressed):

> Now, _fair_ Hip_poly̲ta_,
> our _nup_tial _hour_ Draws _on_ a_pace_;
> four _happy_ _days_
> bring _in_ An_other_ _moon_:
> but, _O_, me_thinks_,
> how _slow_ This _old_ _moon_ _wanes_!

The phrases give these lines their royal tone—they are stately; and the rhythm reinforces the tone—it is a mini-proclamation, slowed at the end by three consecutively stressed syllables. Because of the short phrases, the impression is not of total gravity: Theseus's obvious impatience with a four-day waiting period isn't threatening, just witty (at least for Theseus). Shakespeare was a master of such devices, and the closer you look, the more you see. Young actors easily lose patience if a director spends too much time explaining these things! But rhythm and phrasing are significant parts of Shakespeare's "bottomless-ness," and along about dress rehearsals, some of my actors would begin to notice how much smoother their lines sounded if they used both.

How much should a director insist that student actors strictly follow Shakespeare's iambic pentameter? Younger kids will do better to simply "speak the speech" naturally, conversationally. This is far better than a sing-song effect, or the dreaded "Bardic voice" that so many actors new to Shakespeare use, "bragging to the stars" in a horrible, fakey way. Older actors, however, should definitely be taught the secrets and advantages, so that they will see the difference between this—in "Bardic" —

> To BE, or NOT to be, THAT is the question.

and this, in the correct rhythm:

> To BE, or NOT to BE, that IS the QUEStion.

What a difference. The verbs are now stressed—*NOT to BE, that IS*—finally making this poor trite sentence much more intense and powerful, as it was meant…to be. And the stress on the first part of "question" is a big improvement on the dead ending of the bad version—it leaves that "quest" sound in our minds, so perfect, since all of *Hamlet* is a quest for the truth.

Shakespeare's work is coded with brilliant and useful secrets. The more students know about these secrets, the more they want to know—and the easier it is for them to act out the lines. Here's Macbeth at evening, twisting in the grip of what he has done, and beginning to see the whole world as his evil mirror:

> *Light thickens; and the crow*
> *Makes wing to the rooky wood:*
> *Good things of day begin to droop and drowse;*
> *While night's black agents to their preys do rouse.*

Just those first two words, *"Light thickens,"* conjure up so much. Earlier in the passage, Macbeth paints an image of the coming night destroying the last daylight with its *"bloody and invisible hand."* So first, we think of blood thickening—Duncan's blood, shed by Macbeth himself—spilled blood turning dark: the growing darkness as a mist of blood, thickening and turning darker by the moment. Perhaps we also remember Lady Macbeth's plea to the spirits of evil, to *"make thick my blood."* The idea that even light itself can be violated begins an extraordinary extended image of darkness and threat. Then *"the crow/ Makes wing to the rooky wood"*—I see something like the Hand of Mordor, in crow-shape, dragging a shroud of shadow westward. Not flying, but "making wing"—again, that eerie sense of sorcery and slow malevolence. And "rooky wood"—the one and only time in the entire canon Shakespeare uses the word "rooky"—to mean both "black" and "filled with rooks" (crows). A black bird makes a dark wood even darker. A shred of black cloth joins itself to a larger clot of blackness. And then the last two lines spring the trap: the slowly growing darkness overwhelms/smothers anything good in the world, by waking *"night's black agents"*—the unnamed evil of dark places. Think Pippin in the darkness of Moria, dropping the pebble into the well.

And this is just one small example. Shakespeare's language is so dense, so rich—with meaning and power and emotion—that it can't help but *"sink into your soul,"* as one of my Lady Macbeths said. For my class, staging a play started with the script. It was our guidebook. Many times, Shakespeare uses punctuation to indicate expression—someone might appear to be saying something emotional or exciting, but if no exclamation point is used, the playwright wanted it spoken more matter-of-factly. (Of course, this assumes the punctuation we have in the texts was done by Shakespeare, and not a later editor.) Language is the key to both status—higher status people use "thou" and often speak in poetry, lower class people use "you" and usually speak in prose—and character: compare the self-delusional pomposity of Claudius and Polonius to Hamlet's fumbling yet brilliant honesty.

We read the script over and over, and stopped often to talk about what was happening. Why is Lady Macbeth saying that, and why in that way? The answers to this question helped us see how the scene might look—what she wanted, to whom she spoke, where they were standing, and so on. How does she sound? Is she upset, manipulative, ironic, etc. This is why, ideally, memorizing should always come before blocking. It's so much easier to experiment with how the scene looks when lines are spoken unhesitatingly.

The basics of blocking are fairly simple. Stay downstage as much as possible. Face the audience when speaking whenever you can; if you are speaking to someone on stage, then always "cheat"—i.e., turn slightly toward the audience, instead of speaking sideways (never speak upstage). To avoid monotony, try to use all levels of the stage (floor, seated, standing), and don't speak in a monotone—use dynamics. Always find a lighted spot when speaking: if the audience can't see you, they probably can't hear you. Project your voice so everyone can hear you. (Very rarely did I have to ask a student actor to speak more softly!) Try as much as possible to articulate the words—voice exercises are always good, kids have a tendency to talk too fast and slur their words, but Shakespeare helps. Know when and where to enter and exit. Make eye contact with the person to whom you are speaking. Don't move around or shuffle your feet onstage—instead, find a way to do some "off-point acting" that adds something to the scene—react to what's being said, for instance.

Finally, always try to "step on" your cue line: that is, speak your line immediately after hearing your cue, instead of allowing dead air time. Unless your character needs a moment to think about her response, you should always speak as soon as you are spoken to.

By the time we were ready to try *Macbeth* in 2004, most of these basic staging principles had been internalized by the students coming into my class. Younger kids, whose teachers were now also doing drama, came into my classroom knowing a lot about being onstage, thanks to having had the experience of doing *The Wind in the Willows* or *The Hobbit* in the 3rd/4th class. Also, those classes were always our best audiences—some of them were siblings of my students, and they loved to watch us perform, to get a glimpse of what was ahead for them.

In 2002, I had applied for a grant to help fund the drama program, and I was lucky enough to get $2000 for supporting technology. With some great new lighting equipment, some better quality costumes, and a real fog machine, we were ready to move everything up a notch—and *Macbeth* was the perfect play for it. Two amazing artist-parents spent a week painting a stark Scottish landscape for our backdrop, and the dad, an accomplished carpenter, made us three nest-able black boxes out of heavy-duty plywood. These became our mainstay set pieces—they could be stacked, they could be used on the apron as a mini-thrust platform, and they could turn into everything from tables to tombs.

The first thing they became for us, in the first scene of *Macbeth*, was a bier. Everyone remembers this very brief scene, the three witches meeting in thunder and lightning, setting the dark tone with *"Fair is foul, and foul is fair."* On our stage, the curtain opened on the three boxes, draped in black cloth, supporting a body. Was it dead? Was it Macbeth? We kept it a mystery. Smoky "fog" covered the stage. Above the witches, three red and blue lights shone straight down on the action. Six witches appeared (the traditional parts were doubled), surrounded the body, and began to repeat an ominous chant over it, casting a spell. A scream started the dialogue, which was shared by all of the six. This was accompanied by a hypnotic repetition of *"Macbeth, Macbeth, Macbeth…"* At the end, all six circled the body slowly, chanting the *"Fair is foul"* lines. Curtain.

Many students contributed ideas for this prologue, and we experimented with many versions. In the end, we all felt that it started the play off in just the right way—and it also helped establish the right atmosphere for the actors.

Thanks to our grant, we could afford some other new tricks. One was an internally-lit brazier for the Macbeths' throne room. This was a shallow metal bowl, into which Paul had placed a battery-powered push-light, covered with an orange gel. When Lady Macbeth starts to speak her famous invocation to the spirits of evil —

> *The raven himself is hoarse*
> *That croaks the fatal entrance of Duncan*
> *Under my battlements.*

she picks up the brazier and lifts it high, offering her fiery soul as a sacrifice toward the horrible murder she contemplates. Holding it under her face, in a darkened set, the brazier giving her a witch-like evil glow, she says the famous words that seal Duncan's fate and her own:

> *Come, you spirits*
> *That tend on mortal thoughts, unsex me here,*
> *And fill me from the crown to the toe top-full*
> *Of direst cruelty! Make thick my blood;*
> *Stop up the access and passage to remorse,*
> *That no compunctious visitings of nature*
> *Shake my fell purpose, nor keep peace between*
> *The effect and it!*

Macbeth enters, and their sinister conspiracy begins. Only nine pages into the script, our new technical effects had substantially contributed to setting the foreboding tone of this gruesome story.

In the middle of Act IV, with the main curtains closed while on a small side platform Malcolm and Macduff plan their campaign against Macbeth from England, out came our most effective prop to date—the idea stolen from OSF, of course. Paul had built a faux-stone bowl, about a foot high and three feet across, for the center of the stage. Patsy had filled the plastic liner inside the bowl with a mixture of baby shampoo and red food coloring, giving the contents the perfect look and consistency of human blood.

The following scene is the famous sleepwalking scene. Lady Macbeth, in the grip of guilt and madness over her part in the murder, is trying desperately to wash Duncan's imagined blood from her hands. On our stage, she kneels at the blood bowl, dips in her hands, and scrubs the blood away…with blood, finishing in despair by holding her head in her bloody hands. It was perfect. The words "blood" or "bloody" occur 35 times in this short play—and the effect is like the constant flow from an open wound, it cannot be stanched.

After this scene, our blood bowl remains at the center of the action, becoming—as in Ashland—the source and matter of the combat that follows. In the script, this fighting is symbolized by individual one-on-one duels among the principals of each army. Our actors would appear from opposite sides of the stage and, after challenging each other, lather their hands with the blood and leap into close combat, slapping their hands across each other's white tunics. As at OSF, the effect was much more intense than with sword-fighting. For one thing, because the "blood" didn't stay on their hands forever, fights were relatively quick (compared to sword duels); a couple of grapplings, then a carefully choreographed fall and *coup de grace*. More important was how completely unexpected— and shocking—this kind of fighting was to first-time audiences. Unless you really know what you're doing, swordplay onstage is rarely convincing—especially when the object is to kill someone. This was different: although essentially symbolic, in many ways it looked a lot more real. Best of all, there was much less chance of serious injury to the actors. (In theory at least…but we'll get to that.)

Although we all thought it was a great way to stage the show, practically speaking it was a bit of a nightmare. Even though Paul covered the stage with heavy gray canvas, we still had to spend thirty minutes cleaning it after every show—so as not to give away what would happen. All of the actors' tunics also had to be washed quickly after each performance, to keep the food coloring from setting. We found that it was hard to keep the "blood" out of the actors' eyes when they really got going onstage, but no one had a any serious after-effects. And the smell of the baby shampoo lingered for days. We had a very dedicated group of actors and parent helpers, however, and dealing with these problems together just made us a stronger family.

For the students in my class, *Macbeth* was an exciting challenge. Facing up to the darkness of the play was difficult at first, especially for the three girls who played Lady Macbeth. How could she be so irredeemably evil, and how were they going to show this? We had many circle discussions about what may have motivated her. The realization that both she and her husband were extremely isolated from friendship, or indeed any social connections, first came from the students themselves, and helped them feel their way into her life. Family was so important to our group, they could more easily imagine her descent into madness by envisioning someone totally cut off from it. The group was also fascinated by her reference to nursing a child—what happened to it was both a constant topic of speculation and another possible way to account for her mind-set.

Macbeth the man was another enigma. Even Macbeth himself cannot completely account for his brutality—right after the murder, he praises his victim for being so morally superior. We talked a lot about how he seemed to become schizophrenic—the "dagger of the mind" speech definitely sounds like someone hearing voices. How evil acts create a new persona, and in Macbeth's case, how his wife's taunts pushed him into doing things that only part of him wanted—although whether she was ultimately to blame was the subject of several pretty intense arguments. Quite a few of Shakespeare's greatest creations are actors, pretending to believe certain things, or to act in certain ways, in pursuit of advancement or truth or self-knowledge or status enhancement. Think of Benedick, Rosalind, Bottom, Viola, even King Lear, and the pre-eminent example, Hamlet. Many students recognized the slippery slope of getting caught in a web of lies, and could understand Macbeth's fall in those terms.

The witches, on the other hand, were extremely appealing to my students—so much so, that I decided to double the number in each cast from three to six, and have pairs speak the lines. The witches' prophecies were another great topic for discussion. To what extent did they influence Macbeth's actions? If he thought he was fated to become the king, did that somehow justify what happened? If Macbeth had not murdered Duncan, might he have become King anyway—and how? Were the witches describing the only possible future, or just one of several alternatives? Did their words reflect some spooky essential knowledge of Macbeth's character—and how, since everything we hear about him at the beginning is good? The kids liked to speculate about this stuff, and we spent a lot of time thinking of extra business for the witches to do onstage. The best thing we came up with, in the *"double double, toil and trouble"* scene, was putting baking soda in a goblet on Macbeth's banquet table, so Hecate could pour vinegar into it and create a little foaming fountain, around which she said her spells. The prologue to the play—previously described—was a tribute to the witches' extended presence in our version, as was our epilogue—a candle-lit circle around Macbeth's body, with one final incantation by the whole ensemble.

Once again, we had our share of mishaps during the run. Not because of the famous curse (some of the kids had heard that you're supposed to say "The Scottish Play" instead of *Macbeth*), but because of all the action. This is probably the most action-filled of all the plays: witches stirring cauldrons or making spells, battle scenes, three murder scenes, the unforgettable banquet scene (Banquo's Ghost appearing only to Macbeth), the sleepwalking scene, etc. (And that's another reason why this is a good play to do with students.) With this much going on, things were bound to get congested on a stage as small as ours. Even so, as you will see from the comments, once again the glitches became opportunities for the actors to show their graces.

> *I remember getting our scripts and not understanding the play at first at all. And I was wondering how in the world I could be so many people in one cast. Then we started blocking and it started getting really fun. I remember rehearsing the Porter, and a whole bunch of people laughed and I felt really good. It was really cool when we started doing lights, backdrop, blood bowl, and everything. I remember rehearsing the witches and it just got better and better. Then we started to perform, it was really cool and I felt really involved in what was happening onstage and offstage. It was a really good feeling.*

I remember when there was no blood and I had to say [as Lady Macbeth], *"My hands are of your color but I shame to wear a heart so white." And when R- got the blood in his eyes and just kept on going. My first performance as Lady Macbeth, I was so nervous I thought I was going to die.*

So nervous for the first performance, just pacing up and down and being nervous. And the first time I smelled the blood I thought I was going insane because it smelled so good, then R- told me it was made out of baby shampoo.

I saw the backdrop coming to life as it was being painted. When I saw it with the lights for the first time, it drew me in as I hoped the play would the audience. I remember the smell of the vinegar (the "baboon's blood") that got spilled onstage over and over again, that was a very distinct part of the play for me, a part which I loved.

I was really happy when I got Malcolm, I had a lot of fun doing it. But I felt left out because I didn't get to fight onstage.

In the fight scene when Macbeth and I [Macduff] *were really going at it, we both got hit in the eyes with blood. I remember him hitting me in the mouth, and I tasted the baby shampoo. When he jumped backward to dodge me, he fell and hit the blood bowl. It really hurt him, he could barely walk, but he got up and still said his lines. I was pretty impressed.*

The sound of the drum beating. And seeing the stage with the curtains and lights up, feeling like my character.

I remember breaking the candle in my hand [sleepwalking scene] *but being relieved it still worked. I felt good going on for the bows, the loud cheers cheered me up and made me forget all the mistakes we made.*

*When I smell baby shampoo, I will always remember the blood.
And when I smell vinegar, I will remember that line, "Cool it
with a baboon's blood."*

*When I first saw the backdrop, I felt like I was in Scotland.
When I first heard about Macbeth, I thought it was a Greek
play! But it turned out to be completely different than I thought.
I remember when poor Banquo had to go onstage without
Fleance—but M- did a good job of making it seem like that was
how it was supposed to be.*

*The stinging sensation of blood in my eyes, the taste of blood, the
smell of blood, the feel of blood, and the dripping of blood on the
ground cloth. I remember what Macbeth felt when his wife died,
and when Macduff said he wasn't born of woman, and when
Macbeth died.*

*The stage creaking under my feet, and blood dripping down my
neck. When Hecate jumped onto the boxes, it always scared me
so much, I almost wet my pants! G- would sit in Macbeth's chair
for a minute, then all of a sudden leap out! It was really cool.*

*When we got our scripts, I was like, "Wow! This is going to be
really different!" I was very excited. I remember the strong smell
of baby shampoo, and smoke (fog) rising in the air.*

*When I read what Banquo was saying, I found the "operative
word" in each line to help figure out who he was, by what he was
saying.*

*Getting onstage, the lights in your face, and K- saying "When
shall we three meet again?" in the third scene. So many eyes
staring back at me in amazement. Sitting backstage trying to
get into character, trying to think of how that person feels. Being
scared, and at the same time excited. Having the vinegar spill
over and over. And overhearing the audience comments, good
and bad stuff, but just trying to think, don't let that stop you
from doing your best.*

When I first learned my lines I sort of knew what my characters were like, but I didn't really find out until we started blocking, and I tried things out.

I had this picture of Macbeth when I got the part, but every line and passage I spoke changed the way I looked at him.

In the beginning, they were just people saying lines that made a story. But by dress rehearsal you could tell the other characters' emotions, the actors put more expression into their words.

At first I got my idea of her from the words, then I started getting it from her relationships with other characters. Also by watching how my counterparts played her.

I found the door to my characters by studying their personalities and feelings. For Lady Macbeth's Gentlewoman, her Queen had gone mad, and I thought she must be scared.

At first I didn't understand how important Banquo was. After reading the script and seeing the movies I noticed how important he was, and how he really could have been a threat to Macbeth and his schemes, if Macbeth hadn't killed him.

I finally stopped seeing Macbeth as a mindless murderer and more like a real person. In the "dagger of the mind" speech, I understood that it terrified him.

At first I just said my lines and tried different meanings. But as I thought more and more about the characters, the lines and meanings started coming easier and easier. They would just make sense.

At first I thought, there is NO WAY I am going to be able to do this role [Lady Macbeth]. *But I found out that she and I have a lot in common: if we do something wrong, it comes back and eats us.*

I would be thinking about the lines and how other people said them, and ideas would pop into my head. As Macbeth grew in me, I looked at him differently, in a new light.

At first I thought the witches were, you know, just evil. But they really liked to mess around with people, for fun. They are really weird, and I am still trying to understand them.

When I first got Lady Macbeth I didn't know how to feel. I was afraid I couldn't do it. I didn't know how to be evil. I really wanted to be her, but to be honest I didn't know how. Now in my mind I know who she is and how to be her. The words helped me find her, they were so evil that they helped me. (Also my dad had me watch a Betty Davis movie and it gave me some ideas.)

This play has taught me so much. You don't always have to make people laugh. Macbeth has really changed me as an actress. I have gotten way better at being serious—before this play, I used to laugh when we were practicing, but now I can be serious and not laugh, and it's still fun.

This play really made me look at life. At how people can be so selfish. You really need to cherish life, because you never know what will happen. Don't be selfish! Instead, see how you can improve.

This play has taught me that, like death, telling lies leads on and on. And I used to think more in black and white, now I think more in the gray area, and I think it helps my problem-solving skills.

Doing Macbeth helped me to stop being so self-conscious.

It has made me understand how evil people can be and all the horrible things people sometimes do to hide what they have done.

It has made me realize how powerful some writing can be.
It has also made me feel safer with everyone in class.

I have more self-confidence now, from getting compliments and being recognized more as a person in this class.

I loved the play. I saw it in Ashland and hated it, I didn't want to do it at all. Now I want to keep doing it and keep doing Shakespeare.

With this play I have learned to be able to vent my emotions. And I have learned the true meaning of love, hate, and sadness.

I think it is so cool to have watched these plays when I was in first and second grade, and not know a thing—and to (finally) be doing this and understand everything.

I thought it would be fun and not so different from any other play. It turns out I was wrong. VERY WRONG!. This was the most fun of any play I've ever done.

It was quite interesting to notice, after the shows were over, how different the kids' attitudes were toward the play's tragic theme—and we talked about this in our circles. The success and relief of putting it on seemed to heavily outweigh the horror and evil. Several remarked on how strange it was that while the audience may have left our theater depressed or overwhelmed in some way by all the blood, for the actors themselves the performances were a kind of catharsis (not their word, of course)— they felt as if they had come through the evil and not only survived, but triumphed in some way.

photo by Isabel Gates

Macbeth and Witches. [*Macbeth*]

photo by Isabel Gates

Hamlet in the graveyard. [*Hamlet*]

To Drink Deep Ere You Depart

The class that did *Macbeth* went on to do *MND* in the spring and, the next year, *Much Ado About Nothing*. Six years into intensive theater, my class and Changeling had settled into a nice routine. In class we rehearsed almost every afternoon, the last hour and a half of the day, always ending with a compliment circle. Changeling met twice a week after school for two hours. Many kids who graduated out of my class ended up in Changeling for a play or two or three—usually until middle- or high-school activities prevented it. Some of the kids just couldn't get enough, and the careers of a dozen or so, starting in fifth grade, extended into their senior years. Our alumni, both in and out of Changeling, were also active in community theater, middle and high school drama clubs, and Seattle Children's Theater summer workshops.

In class, we were using the drama program to reach out into our community and to raise funds for the annual trips to Ashland. Large and small groups of actors performed at nursing homes, Rotary Club, in front of supermarkets, in parks, and even on board a Washington State ferry.

Theater and Shakespeare continued to enhance learning in the classroom. Whole-class activities were easier, because the kids were more relaxed and at ease with each other. There was less competition for attention, and petty conflicts were fewer. Getting everyone engaged in community service projects was a lot easier—these were the years when we were doing water-quality monitoring, cleaning streams, and cleaning beaches and parks. Group projects especially were different. As previously noted, working with other ages and genders was easier for kids after trust-building became institutionalized. I saw kids listening to each other better, with more empathy—and more kids reaching out to help those who were struggling academically, or who were having problems at home.

I especially noticed a huge difference in my Creative Writing workshops. We did these once or twice a week; students would write for an hour, then share if they chose to. I noticed a definite jump in the quality of what they were writing about—their subjects were more personal, more real. Theater and trust-building made it easier to share their fears, hopes, anger, and confusion—they knew no one would laugh at them. This in turn made the whole process easier for others to join. Some who were reluctant to share for months eventually felt okay about it, and in the compliment circle afterwards, someone was sure to validate their courage. Similarly, now kids found it easier to invent characters who—like characters onstage—could fight, cry, or act out their inner demons without embarrassing their creators. Over the years, I saved a lot of the writing I liked best, thinking perhaps to put together an anthology someday. After I retired, I couldn't help but notice how much more I started saving in the years beginning about 2002. Some parents believed that doing drama made the kids "more mature." I wasn't too sure about that—I saw plenty of behavior that was still wonderfully (and not so) child-like—typical of adolescence. My own feeling was that playing those roles, finding yourself through being someone else, would better be called intellectual/emotional expansion than "growing up." *"I feel bigger inside"* probably says it even better.

From 2006 to 2008, the tree that was planted in 1999 came to full flower. Our devotion to Shakespeare blossomed. In 2006, the older Options students (grades 6-7-8) put on what still stands as our definitive production of *MND*. I have already quoted many of their feelings about, and responses to, that version. I will add only that its power came from a decision—made early on by the students themselves—to make this the darkest production possible. Our Puck demanded that we incorporate into the set a grave designed for *Hamlet,* into which she "stored" the exhausted lovers; the effect was eerily dreamlike, and the whole show absorbed the subtle malevolence of the fairies toward humankind, giving every scene a nice edge-of-reality flavor. What was usually mere mischief became actual threat, which made the lovers' fears, and the catfight, a bit more desperate than usual. All in all, it was considerably more satisfying than our usual versions.

In the spring of our initial theater year, I had been approached by an outspoken parent (he had two sons in the program, though neither was in my class). After starting the year with *MND*, we had just finished an abridged version of *The Tempest*. "Bob, I heard you're going to do *Hamlet* next," this dad said to me. "Please don't—I beg you! It's my favorite play. These kids are too young, they'll just ruin it." Being relatively new to theater and Shakespeare, up to that point I had simply been thrilled at how excited the kids were, and how, so far, our productions had generally come off fairly smoothly. I hadn't worried that our amateurish-ness might threaten something that someone held dear.

Looking back, I think that his concern was that my students wouldn't—couldn't?—take the play seriously enough to do it justice; that our version would make a mockery of Hamlet's agonized soul-searching, for instance. He may also have been worried that our abridged version would skip through, or even omit entirely, the most famous parts of the text. Fortunately, at that point I didn't know enough to give his concerns too much weight. I told him that I was impressed with what the kids had done so far, and thought they'd probably be suitably respectful of the play, and that we'd hope for the best.

I don't remember his words coming back to me during our early rehearsals, but they should have. For weeks, it did prove difficult for the kids to take the play seriously enough. What 11- or 12-year-old wants to spend a lot of time with Hamlet's level of anxiety, his thoughts of suicide, his obsession with his mother's relationship with Claudius, or with Ophelia's insanity? How do young people—with (thank goodness) little or no experience with these states of mind—identify with characters who are consumed by them?

This was when our trust-building activities began to pay off. Having done two plays together, the kids were pretty solid as a group. In fact, that was what—at first—helped prevent our getting serious. All it took was one cutting one-liner or self-protective sarcastic remark from an actor in a key scene, and the whole group was laughing, relieved that the emotional pressure was off, at least for the moment.

The first threat to this disengagement came from an unlikely source. I had given the role of Laertes to a fifth-grade girl—who, though she had played both Miranda and Thisby, had as yet given little indication of how important drama was to her. One afternoon, we were rehearsing the scene where Laertes confronts Claudius about the death of Polonius (Laertes' father). Nothing much was happening, it was going nowhere. Then, getting a running start from the audience for her entrance, the fifth-grader leaped onto the stage, her sword thrust directly at the King's throat. In a loud and powerful voice, with beautiful expression, she demanded

Oh thou vile king, give me my father!

and everything stopped! Amazed, all the students looked at her and looked at each other. Claudius was too surprised, at first, to respond with his lines. Then, all the kids started clapping and cheering her. After rehearsal, during our circle, the compliments were profuse. Here was someone who had taken a big risk—the risk of looking foolish, even ridiculous, in her enthusiasm, because she believed in the play, in herself, and in her friends—and was rewarded for it. She became an instant hero, and the post-play survey was filled with references to that moment as a turning point in our production.

Things improved. I think the sixth-graders were slightly abashed that a younger student was able to take such a leap, when they were reluctant to get serious. To their credit, they were lavish with their praise, and afterwards I could sense a greater effort from them, especially from the three students playing Hamlet.

Even so, we were still spinning our wheels emotionally in one very important way. Laertes' anger was powerful and inspiring, but the sadness and near-despair of the final scene were proving to be much harder to embody and portray. The Queen, accidentally drinking the poison her husband meant for Hamlet, dies in slow agony while Hamlet and Laertes are fighting a duel. When Hamlet finally notices and reacts, Laertes swipes his arm with a blade "envenomed" with another lethal poison. The duel turns from sport to viciousness. Laertes loses his sword; Hamlet grabs it and wounds Laertes—who, knowing he is about to die, confesses all and implicates the King. Hamlet kills the King by forcing him to drink from Gertrude's poisoned cup, then dies in Horatio's arms.

This scene, probably the most famous in all of English drama, is very intense. Saying the right words while trying to remember where to go and what to do—and trying to sword-fight convincingly at the same time—takes a large amount of concentration and hours of practice. Close to the advent of dress rehearsals, we had all that pretty much down; what we didn't have was the emotional power that makes it all meaningful. Then something trivial happened that changed everything. At the end of one run-through, the boy playing Hamlet—instead of getting up after dying—said into the silence, *"I want to die with my eyes open."*

This was said thoughtfully and seriously. It was so random and unexpected, everything came to a standstill. The statement itself was not really earth-shaking, but more of a simple blocking idea, as in, *"Would this be more Hamlet-like?"* But when the other kids and I heard the first four words, that *"I want to die,"* we heard much more. Wait a minute: someone is actually dying here . . . . . we know it's not our friend T- (playing Hamlet), but . . . . . what if it was? Maybe this wasn't like a movie, maybe this was about a real person dying? And also, we heard that "I" as me/Hamlet. As in, I here and now fully accept this role; I am this person—not ironically, at a distance, protecting myself—but for real. As for the *"with my eyes open"* part, that was also a shocker. Why? Why was that better? *"The rest is silence."*

A bit stunned, and sobered out of their usual playfulness, the class sat and thought about his idea. If it hadn't really registered for most of them how Hamlet, this person they had come to regard as heroic (more on this later), was going to die, and accepted it with grace and courage, now it did. After a short discussion, one of the quietest and most thoughtful talks we'd ever had together, we all decided that yes, that was best. And that after Hamlet dies, when our Horatio speaks those beautiful words —

> *Now cracks a noble heart. Good night, sweet prince,*
> *and flights of angels sing thee to thy rest.*

she would kneel, and very gently, very carefully, using the flat of her hand, close Hamlet's eyes.

So we repeated the scene, putting these new ideas into practice. Everyone watching: no sound, no whispered comments. At the end, a collective sigh of relief and satisfaction. We had found it. This was the key.

From then on, it was a different production. The gravity of that one moment was carried forward into the remaining rehearsals. Ophelia's insanity, and Gertrude's sad tale of Ophelia's death—which had previously been acted superficially, improved measurably. The performances were quite convincing.

After the last show, the outspoken father approached me and apologized. "I saw every cast, every performance," he said. "I cried. The kids were great."

Hamlet came to occupy a special place in our repertory. I never did it again with my 5th/6th class; instead, it became a kind of final exam for every new group of Changelings, the ultimate test of their seriousness and commitment. We did it in 2001, again in 2004, and again in 2007. Each time, it was a little bigger, a little riskier, a little more intense. We experimented with new ways of bringing home the relationships and the themes. We went from our small regular stage to a dramatic thrust stage at another venue, then back home to two facing stages, the action crossing back and forth between them. Our costumes gave the play a vague, late 19th-century look. In one version, we brought Ophelia's ghost back during the final duel, explaining the lapse in Hamlet's actions as his sudden vision of her (slightly offstage, pale white in her wedding gown). We had Ophelia (instead of her father) read Hamlet's letter to her. We brought Hamlet in to act out the strange behaviors she describes to her father. We stole shamelessly from movie versions and from productions we had seen in Ashland and Seattle. As *MND* became the signature play for my class, so *Hamlet* became Changeling's trademark production. Each successive version had actors from the previous version, thus there was the constant challenge of trying to make it different and better, more memorable.

Putting on the most famous play in the English language involves making an agonizing number of difficult choices, starting with the script.

Three different forms of the script exist, with significant differences. Whenever you watch a production of *Hamlet*, you are seeing some director's idea of what he or she thinks should be used from the three versions. And then there are the necessary cuts. Since this is the longest play in the canon, doing it all would require almost four hours. But what to leave out? Like my outspoken friend, someone is bound to be offended. The play has roughly 4200 lines, and one-third of those are Hamlet's. To avoid exhaustion, a director is forced to choose—among many long speeches and soliloquies—the ones he or she thinks best portray the themes and move the action. But when you see a complete *Hamlet*— Kenneth Branagh's film is the best-known—you realize how every word and scene is important to the development of Hamlet's character and plight.

Another difficult range of choices involves the characters. Exactly who is Horatio? If he is Hamlet's best friend, why is there so little dialogue between them? After the early scenes, Horatio all but disappears. He is almost completely helpless to act on, or even speak to, Hamlet's anguish—is this by his own choice, or Hamlet's? Or was the actor who originally played him doubling as someone else in the cast? Gertrude—is she gullible and innocent, or sneaky and guilty? There is considerable evidence for believing both. She is sometimes played as descending into alcoholism—does this make her more pitiable, or less? How is a young woman to play her? And Ophelia—how to show her bizarre behavior to the King and Queen, the combined innocence and bitter cynicism of her insanity, when she seems to see directly into the truth behind all the lies. Very difficult for any actress.

The biggest mystery of all is Hamlet himself. Is he acting crazy, or is he crazy—or does he partly lose his sanity while pretending to? Why is he so brutal to his mother, against the explicit instructions of his father's Ghost—whose demand for revenge he ignores? Why does he have Rosencrantz and Gildenstern executed—and feels not an ounce of pity for them—and why does this matter so little to us the audience? And so on and on, through countless labyrinths of paradox and confusion.

For all we talked about these puzzles, we never solved them—who has? As always, my actors made their decisions based on the relationships that they believed existed among the characters. To them, Hamlet was a hero, trying to find out what was real and what was not, who around him was an authentic person, and who was a phony. In his confusion, his sudden anger, his inability to decide, his defensiveness, his cruelty, his integrity—in all these qualities, they saw their own families, their friends, and themselves, trying to survive with as much dignity and self-knowledge as possible in a world full of lies.

Their favorite scene, consequently, was Hamlet's confrontation with Polonius.

> HAMLET
> Well, God-a-mercy.
> LORD POLONIUS
> Do you know me, my lord?
> HAMLET
> Excellent well; you are a fishmonger.
> LORD POLONIUS
> Not I, my lord.
> HAMLET
> Then I would you were so honest a man.
> LORD POLONIUS
> Honest, my lord!
> HAMLET
> Ay, sir; to be honest, as this world goes, is to be
> one man picked out of ten thousand.
> LORD POLONIUS
> That's very true, my lord.
> HAMLET
> For if the sun breed maggots in a dead dog, being a
> god kissing carrion,—Have you a daughter?
> LORD POLONIUS
> I have, my lord.
> HAMLET
> Let her not walk in the sun: conception is a
> blessing: but not as your daughter may conceive.
> Friend, look to it.

LORD POLONIUS

[Aside] How say you by that? Still harping on my
daughter: yet he knew me not at first; he said I
was a fishmonger: he is far gone, far gone: and
truly in my youth I suffered much extremity for
love; very near this. I'll speak to him again.
What do you read, my lord?
HAMLET
Words, words, words.

For them, this was the epitome of Hamlet-ness, this incredibly cool, sarcastic put-down of someone who had no clue. Fascinated by theater and the various possibilities of self-creation through acting, they loved it that Hamlet's whole persona was an act, that he acted out so many different roles so well, and that in doing so he finally found out who he was, and in the end was able to let go of all his confusion and indecision and just...act. Each time we did the play, the actors seemed to find acting itself as the best way to come to terms with *Hamlet*.

Getting to that point, however—learning to immerse themselves in something so ambiguous and complex—was quite a journey, and as evidence, I want to offer some of the trials and challenges this play involved for the actors in their own words. It was always a struggle. Auditions held more anxiety: since this was the ultimate way to test yourself in our world, picking the role that was right for you—without stepping on a friend's toes—was crucial. Rehearsals were sometimes nightmarish—because everyone had other things going on, because so many lines had to be memorized, because the blocking was difficult, because it was *Hamlet*. Since this was an after-school group, trust was not built-in, as it was in the classroom, but had to be rebuilt at every meeting, and was often fragile until the performances. Most of the time, we were dress-rehearsing in borrowed spaces, meaning we had to take down the set every evening and re-set it the next day. In addition, the disconnect between this play (and its main character) and the circumstances of their daily lives was sometimes disconcerting.

I remember sitting around not knowing what I was doing,
listening to K- raving about how the other play she was in
was so annoying. Memorizing for hours. Doing the closet
scene out on the lawn while one of my other teachers watched
and tried to ruin it with his sarcasm.

I remember setting up the set and taking it down every day.
It seemed like every time we did it the stage pieces got lighter
and lighter.

When we were practicing we couldn't seem to pull it together,
we would read our lines okay, but nobody memorized, or only
a few. We had fun sometimes, but most people couldn't pull
it together, and some people quit.

Rehearsals were a disaster. Where's J-? He's with M- and D-,
filming a movie for school—during rehearsal. Where's C?
He didn't bring a snack and was hungry, so he went home.
We'd sit around and talk about being committed and not let-
ting each other down. I felt responsible but I didn't know what
to do.

Two weeks before the performance we had a session of "baby-
killing." Baby-killing consisted of the cast sitting in a circle
and discussing character cuts because people weren't memorized
and we were running out of time. People were going to have to
give up major roles. H- and J- gave up Laertes to do Polonius.
M- gave up Claudius, and just did Ophelia and Ghost. The big-
gest decision came when R- dropped out of the role of Hamlet.
He knew that he could not get memorized in time and gave all
the casts to me. Ultimate sacrifices were made in that circle. We
all sighed with relief afterwards, but I know there are people who
have regrets.

C- was the youngest in the cast, the most inexperienced, and the
most spacey. He rarely attended rehearsals, and when he did he

made paper-clip chains and ate chips in the back. He was cast as the priest—a total of six lines—and was not memorized. When he got on the stage I immediately saw the talkative fifth-grader become introverted and insecure. His shoulders drooped and his eyes cast down as if trying to hide. His words were mumbled and he would not make eye contact with Laertes as they walked toward the grave.

Eventually, because they all knew that their close friends were depending on them, everyone put the time in, and the play came together—at the last possible minute. As always, it wasn't threats or the promise of rewards, but the actors' own strong sense of solidarity and trust that made it happen.

The night before opening I took C- aside. I said, you have no reason to be nervous. You're in this cast for a reason. We need you to be confident, enunciate. Ophelia killed herself, you can't give her a proper burial, and Laertes won't leave you alone. Don't be afraid to get angry. Let it out! When opening night came, Horatio and I were crouched at the side of the stage as the funeral procession came through. "What ceremony else?" Laertes said. C- looked right at me in the shadows. I gave him a quick smile and he projected, "Her obsequies have been as far enlarged as we have warranted." At the end of the scene, I rushed backstage to congratulate him. He was beaming.

I remember feeling really dizzy and sick right before we went onstage. I didn't feel ready to go on, and then right when we were about to go on I was picked up and squeezed, I looked behind me and it was A-! Then I went onstage and the rest was silence.

I was standing backstage, feeling sick to my stomach. I had a headache, my nose was all stuffed up and made me talk funny. I thought I was gonna walk onstage and collapse (how

*embarrassing). But I stepped up into the light. Everyone
watched. I said my first line. I didn't sound funny. I continued.
My stomach felt better. I was into it. I felt like a king who had
just been elected.* [He was Claudius.] *I was thrilled. It was
magic. I remember everyone being SO into character. One of
the nights, I thought Laertes was really gonna kill me!*

*The first performance, last scene, when Hamlet and Laertes
were dying, I was so wrapped up in it that I was close to tears.
I was like that for both of the other shows, too.*

*We pulled it together so well for the performances. Everybody
got so into character and we did great. J- as the Gravedigger
was so funny, but K-* [Hamlet] *didn't crack up. Claudius was
evil. Rosencrantz became a frat boy! Ophelia got so crazy the
audience was scared.*

*Opening night was SO GOOD compared to what we were
expecting (or at least what I was). The second performance
always sucks, people never have the same energy. Anyway,
Saturday night, magical again. M- as Ophelia, in the crazy
scene, she had people in tears. She was absolutely incredible
going crazy and in the nunnery scene. The closet scene
between me and Gertrude was also great—and the table!
I attacked her and knocked the table over, but I caught it
in mid-air and set it up again while screaming at her. It was
very hilarious. But that was also a great scene.*

*Just the intensity of the whole thing, especially Saturday
night. The excitement/nervousness every time I looked
around at the people onstage—no doubts, just excitement!
Gosh, so emotional, the Ophelia crazy scene, the willow
speech, the chapel scene. Endless days of rehearsal and worry
about "Will this ever work?"—but from the first minute of
the first scene on the first night, I knew it would be a big hit.*

The hardest part, for me, was discovering Guildenstern. His character is very hard to understand, and to play. He's such an empty shell and cardboard cut-out, that playing him is difficult, I've never played a part quite like it. But I couldn't have understood him without help from cast members, especially K-, who seemed to be struggling with Rosencrantz too.

I asked the actors what they learned from doing the play. As usual, some of their answers were about the content of the text, but others were more about their own personal experience as a member of the cast.

That Hamlet is so much more than a guy holding a skull and saying a bunch of famous lines. That we are capable of so much more than any of us thought. That we could become so close, so together, that we could all get this together in about three days.

I learned how to change again, and to love. I learned I'm not all I thought I was, in a way that is hard to understand if you are not me.

At the beginning of the year I was falling into this place where I didn't care about acting. It was terrible, but it felt normal. Then, performing Hamlet showed how much I NEED to act. Acting is part of me, no matter how far it gets pushed down.

I learned that you can't have a performance without working together. That even the small, small parts are needed. And that if one thing goes wrong, everyone has to be really connected to pull it off.

I learned that there are more important things to life than schoolwork or money. For a while I thought of earth as a marble covered with germs. During the dark months of winter I almost thought that what I did was pointless, cause I was a little germ in the whole scheme of things. But then I realized how dumb I was for believing that. So what if we are all just little germs. Just do what you do to make yourself happy. That's all that matters in this world. "What is this quintessence of dust?"

I'm still finding things out for myself. But I have grown up a bit with this play, I realized that even I have faults that I need to address.

I have learned so much from this play, doing it, becoming it. I got a lot older by doing this. This play taught me to trust the cast even more than I already did. I finally got it, how far people would go. How much I myself could do, that I never knew I could do—like be sad, act in a way I never had before.

I felt a new appreciation for the play. I never thought it could be so powerful. From being in it, I feel very different. I have opened up to myself and to other people. I have become much happier. I feel very free, invincible. I was skeptical at first—I didn't realize it would be like that.

It kept me going this past month. Being able to get all my emotions out, being able to yell "God have mercy on his soul!" What I was really saying inside was, "I hate math with Ms. ___!" Being able to let go of all my stuff inside. That's what really got me through. It reminded me not to worry about every little thing, that it would be all right.

This is so hard. There are so many personalities to relate it to. Hamlet is confusion—love, hate, love again. Hamlet is a lifetime in five acts. With all the dirty parts. Everyone has a part for them, even if they don't know it yet.

It means a lot. Most of all, I feel that I can relate to Hamlet sometimes—there are things in the world that cannot be solved, but are so unbearable that you cannot let them pass without trying to do something.

I am so glad for this play. This play keeps me going. It's the reason I still get up in the morning. School starts at 7:30 and ends at 3:30—that's 8 hours. But with Hamlet awaiting my arrival, I put up with it all. This play lets me release all my hate and anger into a character, who has consumed me. I dream about it at night. It's a strong belt that holds us all together. The play is almost like water. If I go too long without it, I can get dehydrated and collapse. And with too much, I get intoxicated with it and forget everything. I go into a daze, but it's good. I love getting drunk off of Shakespeare.

Hard work. Acrobatic tendencies. Meeting of minds. Love for all the players. Emotion from all. Totally perfect.

Hamlet is strange. There are a lot of lonely people in it, but by doing it you bring people together. It's about truth. It is very good to do to help yourself.

I am a changed person. It was incredible. It really was.

I felt something—I don't know what, but I feel funny now, different. I threw so much of myself into that role, that—I don't know. I think I actually pulled this one off. I've never been happy with the way I did Ophelia three years ago. And I've had my doubts about Puck and Flavia (in Noises Off). But this one, I feel like I really gave it everything I had and feel…clean? It was just, wow. I actually did it. It's weird. I don't know.

In the beginning, I remember clumsily going through the motions, attempting to say the overwhelmingly confusing words, and being pushed onstage into a world of unknown emotions and fears. Yet this experience helped me get in touch with myself as a person. Every time I immerse myself in my character, I am shocked by the blast of the reality I am faced with. I love it.

The role of Claudius has challenged me to look deeply into the darkest sides of the human soul, and in so doing, I have learned that within the soul is an endless capacity for emotion, as well as an infinite number of choices available to us.

Working with all of my fellow actors has been an amazing experience, and I will always treasure it. Playing Gertrude has been different from many of my other parts because she is so understated; finding her has been a challenge that I have relished.

Doing Hamlet is an intense experience. Being Ophelia has shown me how much freedom I have. When Ophelia goes crazy, she shows what happens in a society where love and grief are not truly allowed. Hamlet is a fight between the heart and what is perceived—what is acted on because of perception, not because of truth and feeling. I think that the play is meant to hit you hard, to slap you and wake you up. I hope the truth of our feeling did it justice.

The 2007 version of *Hamlet* was different from our previous productions—and from almost all productions—in one very significant way: the lead role was played by a young woman. Since entering my class as a fifth-grader in the fall of 2001, this student had been intensely passionate about Shakespeare and theater. She played many important roles in her two years there, then went on to play Rosencrantz and, three years later, Ophelia in the Changeling productions. An excellent actress, she loved the challenge of making Shakespeare come alive. I think she knew from the start that she was meant to play Hamlet, and she refused to let stereotypes or prejudice get in the way. As she wrote in her program bio, *"Our search for the truth in*

ourselves knows no gender." As a pioneer of sorts, and since she went on to
do even greater things after the 2007 *Hamlet,* in some ways she personified
what our whole theater program came to mean, and I want to quote at
length from her reflections on that production.

> *Somehow I guess I knew that I was to play Hamlet. It was
> casually suggested many times in the past years and it marinated
> in my brain for a long time. I wasn't ready, but I was ready to
> try. Most of the senior cast was gone, so for the first time I was the
> experienced one. I was the person who intimidated me years ago.
> Before rehearsals even started, I vowed not to be like the previous
> Hamlet. I did not want my Hamlet to be admired from afar or
> idolized on a pedestal. I would build a relationship with everyone
> in the cast, no matter how young, scared, or inexperienced. And
> for that, we would be stronger. For it to work, there needed to be
> trust. I didn't know what that meant at the time, but vowed to
> put everything I had into Hamlet, the man and the play.*
>
> *It's hard to explain my love for the stage. Before Hamlet,
> I could say it was because of the energy and pay-off of working
> hard for months to put a show together. Hamlet had all these
> aspects for me, but I learned something else, too. It was about a
> message. They didn't know it, but the audience needed to see it
> just as much as I needed to perform it.*
>
> *The show was being cast before auditions were even
> announced. In our tight group, we knew each other's capabili-
> ties. The cast was scribbled on the back of a script in the car
> on the way back from the Oregon Shakespeare Festival. We
> spent hours putting casts together by chemistry and experience.
> Auditions were held and. surprisingly, minds were changed. We
> talked for hours and sent countless emails. Finally the cast was
> set and we all looked at each other and said, Here we go again.*
>
> *Rehearsals were terrible until C-, who had been Change-
> ling's original assistant director, came back from art school in
> Michigan to work with us. For her, acting was life. She lived it,
> breathed it, loved it. This is why she inspired me, but it is also
> why I was terrified of her when she got in that mindset. One*

*freezing December night, she took us outside to the undercover
area of the playground and ran us through countless exercises. I
recited "Oh that this too too sullied flesh would melt"—because
it was the only speech I knew—a hundred different ways. C- had
us walk like our characters, walk like other people's characters,
and interact with each other. She taught us some stage combat
and made people focus. She got us thinking, feeling, and finally
doing. All this before anyone was even close to being memorized.*

*C- went back to school. We went back to rehearsing inside.
But now something had changed. People were serious! I had been
so frustrated, throwing myself into this with no one following me,
and now I realized that I hadn't even begun. As my cast members became more involved, I found myself delving deeper and
deeper into Hamlet's psyche. I analyzed the lines, but not like I
had done with Ophelia. I made notes so I could understand every
single word. I started portraying Hamlet in a different way than
we had done him before, in a way that was new even to our director. I would try something onstage and Bob would go, "Whoa!
Keep that. I've never seen that before, it was great!" Or, "I'm
not so sure I like that. Why did you do that? Does Hamlet think
Gertrude knows Claudius killed his father?" When I didn't have
an answer, we would discuss it. I was forced to plunge deeper.*

*Finally we decided on the set. It was an ingenious cross-
shaped stage. I had never acted in the round before, but I found
it surprisingly natural to turn in all directions and use the entire
room. Laertes and I fenced on a lower level in the middle of everyone, making sure to avoid the audience's heads when we swung
for a hit. The grave was at one end, the court at the other, and I
got to use all of it. It's more believable to go crazy all over the room
instead of standing on a box. Boxes make crazy people crazy.*

*M- was my Ophelia. She was quiet and awkward, but she
also inspired me. I knew from the beginning that she and her
brother, also in the cast, had been through a lot. M- had been
deeply scarred, and I wondered if Ophelia would help her or hurt
her even more. Then it started. I have never witnessed anyone
throw themselves more completely into a role than M- did. She*

was Ophelia. "He is gone, he is gone/ and we cast away moan/ God have mercy on his soul." I was in tears. <u>We were stunned.</u> It was real. When she left the stage and exited into the hallway on closing night, J- followed her out. Backstage, J- started talking to D- and they turned to look at M-. She was still in character. As I watched from the other side of the stage, J- put his hand on her shoulder and she violently shook him off. She was still crazy. She was wild and childlike backstage, pacing and occasionally whispering to herself. I was shocked. M- was Ophelia when no one was watching! M- was Ophelia until the last blackout—maybe longer.

It's always hard to remember opening night. Adrenaline gives me short-term memory loss. I remember D-—I mean Claudius—giving me my first cue. "A little more than kin and less than kind" came out strong. My voice was powerful, even though my knees were not. I remember attacking Gertrude, who was almost in tears. I remember saying the last part of "but the dread of something after death" to Ophelia. I remember fencing perfectly, and how I felt like crying when Horatio said "this nothing's more than matter."

Then there was the pause.

The pause is the reason Hamlet is so important. It is the reason Shakespeare is still being performed after hundreds of years. After the last line is spoken, after the last drum beat, after the lights go down, if your show is good, there is a pause. The audience does not erupt into applause, they wait. Soak in the moment. That moment, of complete silence, means that you have affected the audience in a way they did not know was possible. As I lay on the stage, hand outstretched to Horatio, my family lying dead around me, I heard the pause. I had thrown myself off the deep end, in hopes of being caught. This moment, held in the air by all of us, by cast and crew, by C- in Michigan, by J- who was Hamlet before me, was the net that saved me.

Even after doing the play four times, I could not get over how immediately it spoke to the students, the audience, all of us. How was it possible, I remember wondering, for anyone to think that Hamlet was about indecision and vacillation?

> *But heaven hath pleased it so,*
> *To punish me with this, and this with me,*
> *That I must be their scourge and minister.*

At the core of this play, written over 400 years ago, is one person's burning need to see and tell the truth. And to proclaim the truth in a voice of prophecy and seeming madness. And to follow the destiny of that truth all the way to its unavoidable consequence. A "scourge" is a whip, and to see/hear this play rightly—as one of the actors said above—is to feel the slap of Shakespeare's whip-like words. This is not a play about ideas or abstractions. It is a play about righteous anger, and blood, and poison, and madness, and acceptance, and forgiveness, and speaking the horrible truth. It is not a logic puzzle, nor a collection of famous lines. It is a passion play, as enacted daily in the moral lives of each of us. It was in that sense of challenge that we performed it, always trying to live up to our motto, as printed in the program: *"We will teach you to drink deep ere you depart."*

> *I think the level we did this play on was so high, we*
> *couldn't have changed it to make it any better. I*
> *thought it was incredible.*

> *I'll never forget how we captured the audience and*
> *sucked them into Hamlet's insane world. I won't forget*
> *the wave from the center when Ophelia screamed.*

> *I will always remember the feeling of family. We were*
> *together, and that is a truly amazing feeling.*

> *At the end. When Horatio put the King's crown on*
> *Hamlet's dead body. I've always thought that was a*
> *perfect way to end the play. That was the perfect touch.*

After this production, with its feeling of bringing us full circle to a kind of closure on *Hamlet*, I believed we had done the play for the last time. Which shows how little I knew. But more of that later.

If This Be Magic

One of the most rewarding things about doing theater with young people was watching them surprise themselves. Several of the survey selections I have quoted mention this, and because of the high value I placed on it, it was a common topic at student conferences. I often asked them to tell me what they did that caused the reaction, how they felt about it, and what they thought it meant for their own development.

Surprise is an underrated emotion. I like the conciseness of the Wikipedia summary: "Surprise represents the difference between expectations and reality." In our culture, it seems to all but disappear in many adolescents—either because media have over-exposed them to "reality," or because they have been socialized to have few expectations, or both. To hear them admit to such a variety of surprises from their theater experiences was always encouraging.

For one thing, surprise is an important element in any kind of real learning. When we are startled by our ignorance, it can create an opening for new ideas, or even new paradigms. Furthermore, surprise seems to be character-building. *"I'm not who I thought I was"* was one student's surprised response to his theater experience, and other comments on the surveys indicated similar reactions, along the lines of, *"I proved that I could do it"*—or even, *"I know that I can do better."* Sometimes, surprise makes us drop our usual defensiveness, which can lead to positive emotional developments: think of the popular boy in an earlier chapter, who surprised himself by acknowledging his long-alienated friend.

Many things about our productions surprised my students, but Shakespeare was the dominant agent of change. Coming in with little actual knowledge of his work, and burdened with the image of something heavy and unintelligible, they found the reality of his words—especially as acted out—fascinating and even exciting. Just as unexpected was their own new-found ability to understand and perform those words, and the resulting boost in self-confidence.

Trust-building was another surprise. Each class entered filled with doubt that they could achieve the kind of bond that had energized the previous class. And yet, through the trust activities, each class managed to get there.

The many ways in which my actors surprised themselves taught me a lot about the nature of creativity, and how drama is so successful at fostering it. A poet and creative writing teacher I know once said to me, "The poems I write that I end up liking best are the ones where I surprised myself." Surprise and creativity seem to go hand-in-hand: the most exciting imaginative leaps and discoveries are the ones that seem to come out of nowhere, that shock or startle us into new ways of self-expression. My students sometimes found themselves speaking Shakespeare's lines at home, in response to something a parent or sibling said. More often, onstage, saying a line they had said dozens of times before, they would make a sudden cognitive and/or emotional jump, a sudden realization about what something meant, or why someone acted in a certain way, that was like getting an electric shock. The sixth-grade girl playing the drunken butler Stephano in *The Tempest*, instead of trying to weave around or slur her speech, suddenly simply collapsed and said her next lines while flat on the floor—it was completely unplanned and totally hilarious. In one of our final versions of MND, during the Pyramus and Thisby scene, Bottom threw a wineglass into the audience, and Peter Quince suddenly walked into the first row, apologizing for Bottom's behavior, and declared his intention of selling the wineglass on eBay. The sudden revelations we had about Hamlet's personality would fill their own chapter. The best one, for me, was during one rehearsal when our Hamlet realized that the visiting players were—except for Horatio—his only true friends, and began relating to them in a totally new way.

Because our program promoted extensive contact between teachers and parents, I often heard the actors' parents express surprise at what they saw onstage. Some of this was a natural result of seeing their son or daughter in a strange costume, of course. (The sight of your 12-year-old daughter appearing onstage in a full-length wedding gown—as Hero in *Much Ado*—was a guaranteed shocker.) Hearing Elizabethan words and rhythms coming out of their kids' mouths could be a bit surprising, if they hadn't heard any out-loud memorizing at home. But the real revelation, for many, was seeing new and different facets of their student's personality appear from (seemingly) nowhere. Naturally believing that by the time their daughter was 12 or 13 they had a good grasp of who she was, parents were startled to see her confidently playing a girl pretending to be a boy who is pretending to be a girl (as Rosalind in *As You Like It*); or intensely portraying a deranged murderess queen (Lady Macbeth); or acting the part of a dead young mother, desperately trying to relive her twelfth birthday before she goes to her grave (Emily in *Our Town*). "Where did THAT come from?"—I heard this quite a bit. Watching parents look at a son or daughter with new respect after the show was worth a lot, especially if I knew there had been issues in the family. Surprise in all its varieties—positive and negative—was our constant companion.

The most surprising play we did was the one with the very un-Shakespeare-like surprise ending. At the end of his career, Shakespeare turned away from the bitterness and brutal tragedy of *Lear* and *Othello* to a genre of plays we now call romances—because while they definitely aren't tragic, they're not really comedy, either. His grand and ethereal *Tempest* is the best-known of these plays, but the strangest, and in many ways the most fulfilling, is *The Winter's Tale*. That the Changelings agreed to put it on in the first place, that our casts changed so many times, and that we actually performed it effectively without a single complete run-through in rehearsal—all these were part of the surprise package it turned out to be.

The story of *The Winter's Tale* moves between the court of King Leontes in Sicilia and the country of Bohemia, where Polixenes rules. Polixenes' long visit to his close friend's kingdom ends badly, when Leontes is suddenly possessed by a jealous madness. He convinces himself that his pregnant Queen, Hermione, is having Polixenes' child. Leontes banishes Hermione's newborn daughter, Perdita, but Hermione is cleared at trial by the Oracle of Delphi. Exhausted by childbirth, overwhelmed by the banishment of her baby and the subsequent death of her son Mamillius, Hermione faints and is carried away. Her death is announced to the court by her good friend Paulina. Far away, baby Perdita is found and adopted by an unlikely father, a Bohemian shepherd.

The second half of the story picks up 16 years later. Perdita, unaware of her royal parentage, falls in love with Polixenes' son, Prince Florizel. Polixenes finds out, and when he objects to their engagement because he thinks Perdita is a lowly shepherd girl, the couple flees to Sicilia. Strangely, the reconciliation of all these entanglements doesn't happen onstage, but is related second-hand by witnesses. What does occur onstage, at the very end, is the magical and startling "rebirth" of Hermione, and her reunion with her husband and lost daughter.

For many special reasons, *Hamlet* is the play that best symbolizes our whole theater project, for me. But as far as which play gave us all the most emotional satisfaction, it will always be *The Winter's Tale*. Is the plot unbelievable and fantastic? Of course. Is the story melodramatic? Yes—but in a good way: after all, the great Robertson Davies himself (drama critic as well as novelist) defended melodrama as, unlike tragedy and comedy, representing "the world we actually live in." Is it really, as many critics and scholars insist, two plays cobbled together—the first half tragedy and the second half comedy? Well, perhaps—but the very same thing could be said of *As You Like It*. Is it intensely exciting, and powerful, and does it contain several of the best scenes he ever wrote? Yes, yes, and yes. Does it feature the strongest female character Shakespeare ever created, whose fiery defense of her closest friend—and whose magical restoration of the friend to life—are without parallel in the canon? Absolutely.

For the Changeling actors who did *Hamlet* in 2007, *Winter's Tale* was their swan song. After years of Shakespeare, the young people who played Hamlet, Gertrude, Claudius, Laertes, Horatio, and Ophelia were moving on, and they wanted to leave their mark with one last memorable production. *Winter's Tale* seemed a perfect fit, filled as it was with roles that embodied passionate jealousy (Leontes), passionate loyalty and integrity (Paulina, Hermione, Perdita, and Florizel), and passionate foolishness (the famous rogue Autolycus). Once again, we had enough actors for two casts. Once again, there was lots of friendly negotiating and trading of roles. After deciding what the script should look like, we were off.

Or so we thought. From the first week, problems popped up everywhere—and the worst was scheduling rehearsals. We had dealt with practice interruptions before, but never like this. Some of the kids were doing soccer or softball—often, with coaches who said, "Miss one practice and you're gone!" They were doing other plays at other schools. Dance classes. Swim team. Some had after-school jobs. They were all committed to the play, but real life kept surprising their (and my) expectations.

We struggled and struggled. Convinced it wasn't going to happen, several kids stopped memorizing. There was little anger—we all realized we were victims of circumstance, and no one tried to blame those who couldn't show up. A month before show-time, things looked really bleak. Three kids—or was it four?—dropped out.

Then, as happened several years earlier, two younger actors came to our rescue. One of the dropouts, a girl whose mother had recently died, and who was struggling with depression, decided to come back. With the support and encouragement of her friends in the cast, she began to get into her role—and inspired the others. Two weeks before performances, an eighth-grade boy decided to join us as a replacement for one of the leads—Leontes. His incredible energy and passion for the play—he memorized his huge part in only 10 days—jump-started us for the big finish.

In addition to these small miracles, many of the cast began to realize how important the play was for the shy high school student playing Hermione. A- had never before had such a big role, and she saw this one as her last chance to prove to herself that she could get past her fear. Loved and admired by everyone in both casts, she would never have put herself forward as a reason for us to keep going. The kids knew, however, and her brave effort to overcome her anxiety became another inspiration.

With one of the simplest sets ever, with very basic costumes and props, we opened. Leontes watched his best friend talking to his pregnant wife, and shocked himself and the audience by suddenly transforming into a jealous psychopath. The play was on, everyone in the cast biting their nails, wondering how on earth we could get through it with so little rehearsal time behind us. But we did. The audience was suitably surprised—by the intensity of the actors, and by the amazing ending. The cast was stunned by their success, which they had no reason to believe was possible. But no one was more surprised than the director.

I remember M- coming up to me before the first show and she was really nervous, so we breathed together — 5 in, 5 hold, 5 out.

I remember not getting memorized until the day of performance. And running my lines while Leontes was talking onstage.

I was more nervous for this play than I've ever been for any other play. Before the first performance I was thoroughly convinced I was going to be sick. But then I went onstage and, as always, it was peaceful. Also, I remember all the crazy cast switches. Just looking at the "revised" cast list and laughing.

Messing up so bad in rehearsal. Worried about not being memorized. Finally getting it right in performance.

It started off kinda slow....and kept being slow, right up until two weeks before the first show. Then we climbed to the top of the mountain, and slid down through the performances. They worked well, just as I thought they would, but I was kinda worried. I mean, most plays I've done, we were always pulling it together at the last minute, but at least we'd have one run-through. We didn't even have one of those for this one, but it still worked.

Memories: A- to the rescue as Leontes. Baby-killing once again. Autolycus stealing Shepherd's coat and wallet. Performing scenes we never rehearsed! Kissing the donkey (last time!) again at casting. Bob: "You really want to be

*the director, don't you?" M- as Hermione, breaking down
at the death of Mamillius. J- as Leontes, ripping off his
jacket during the "what studied torments" speech, truly
crazy. T-'s perfect voice for Mamillius. Perdita's facial
expressions, genuine and so real. Our many creative
renditions, it was like a different show every time! A- as
Hermione at the end, her freezing cold nervous hand, and
J- as Leontes saying "Oh, she's warm!" anyway. Embarrassing post-show speeches [it was her final play]—but
really appreciating it at the same time. Crying (damn, I
knew this was going to happen!) and R- hugging me
(thanks, pal).*

*K- and M- as Paulina, screaming at Leontes. J- as Auto-
lycus, saying, "Oh, that fish! That fish!". S- as Shepherd,
making sheep noises and humming!! Brilliant!!*

Exiting the stage and feeling so good.

*When Perdita and I [Florizel] turned to look at each other
at the same moment and smacked our faces together. It
was good because we started laughing at the perfect moment,
when the others were saying, "He tells her something."*

*Best moment? All of Saturday night's show. I had so much
fun. And it was perfect.*

*Saturday night's performance, the last scene. Leontes
looked up at the sky with a look of true happiness on
his face.*

*In every play I have acted in, my characters have helped
me become something more than I was before. Paulina
encourages me to say what needs to be said. Hermione
reminds me that what needs to happen in the end will*

happen. This play is wonderful. It shows me that no matter how harsh the winter, spring will come and fix whatever has been broken.

To the whole cast—I don't think many of you know how much you all mean to me. Like it or not, we have now bonded in an unbreakable way. You have all seen a piece of my soul and I hope you have shared a piece of yours with me. Thank you for everything. I need you all and will remember you forever and always.

After the Saturday night show my mom said there were times when she forgot I was a girl. She said it creeped her out.

In the end, love will prevail. Love and forgiveness, those were the big things I took from the play.

Love is not bound by the rules some give it. And don't jump to conclusions before you have all the facts. But really, words can't describe what I feel about this play and what it meant. It's a feeling that has no words.

There are so many messages in this play. Respect, forgiveness, the power of love and jealousy. You can always forgive someone, no matter what, even if it takes 16 years.

It made me want to fix what has been wrong and broken in my own life.

How did we manage to pull it off, when we were discussing the blocking the day of the performance?

Ha! I might say I was surprised that we pulled it off, but really I'm not. I knew we could do it.

I will never forget how I got chills down my spine every
time Paulina said the "What studied torments, tyrant,
hast for me?" speech. I don't think I'll ever really forget
this group of people, coming together to breathe life into
these characters and bring this story back in a unique and
beautiful way.

The onset of Leontes' jealous madness in the first part of *Winter's Tale* is so startling, like anything monstrous inside of us of which we are not aware. But just as surprising, for a Shakespeare play—or any Elizabethan play, was Paulina's incredible rage when she calls him on it:

> *What studied torments, tyrant, hast for me?*
> *What wheels? racks? fires? what flaying? boiling?*
> *In leads or oils? what old or newer torture*
> *Must I receive, whose every word deserves*
> *To taste of thy most worst? Thy tyranny*
> *Together working with thy jealousies,*
> *Fancies too weak for boys, too green and idle*
> *For girls of nine, O, think what they have done*
> *And then run mad indeed, stark mad! For all*
> *Thy by-gone fooleries were but spices of it.*

The fact that his jealousy, the chaos and death it caused, and her righteous rage (against a King—this was treason) could all be forgiven in the end, this was the message my actors carried away. When Paulina brings Hermione's "statue" to life in the last scene with those amazing words—

> *Tis time; descend; be stone no more; approach;*
> *Strike all that look upon with marvel. Come,*
> *I'll fill your grave up: stir, nay, come away,*
> *Bequeath to death your numbness, for from him*
> *Dear life redeems you.*

it was as if each one of them had been reborn. Never before or since have I seen a cast more exhilarated at the end of a performance. Not just because they actually did it—though relief was certainly a big part of their reaction to the first show—but even after succeeding shows, they were glowing with happiness.

The Winter's Tale is Shakespeare's "yes" to life. It is his summing up, his final answer, to all the riddles and questions. Yes, people do horrible, irrational, cruel things to each other. Yes, even in the face of divine correction, the powerful sometimes (always?) insist that their truth is the only truth. Yes, the consequences are invariably tragic.

But yes, everyone is redeemable. Yes, the love we have for each other sometimes (always) insists that humanity will prevail. Yes, wholeness is possible. Death is always balanced by creation, by imagination, by humor, by love's intense integrity, by forgiveness and reconciliation, by the long faithfulness of our belief in each other.

Hermione, Paulina, Mamillius, and Emilia. [*The Winter's Tale*]

The Tie That Binds

It is a commonplace of Bardolatry (the superficial worship of "Shakespeare the Genius") that his plays contain the universe—every personality type, character trait, state of mind, obsession, emotion, virtue, historical period, geographical locale, flower, animal, etc. that the early Renaissance world offered to his view. While there is a certain kind of metaphorical truth to this claim, it is interesting to consider the things he never wrote about—or, some say, went out of his way to avoid.

One was happy marriages. There aren't any. There are plenty of joyous weddings; but happily married couples, living contented lives of faithfulness and devotion? Not a one. There are numerous virtuous fathers—Leonato, Duke Senior, the Shepherd in *The Winter's Tale*, Prospero—but where are their wives? Gone, or non-existent. Oh yes—perhaps the Macbeths? They seem to come the closest, and what does that tell us? Of course, biographers have had a field day with this. Shakespeare's relationship with his wife remains one of the great mysteries. Then again, perhaps happy marriages were simply too dull for him to make use of.

Another omission that stands out is everyday small town and village life. We're usually either in court, in the forest, on the battlefield, at sea, on an island, on the road, in the city, in a castle, on the heath, or in a palace. The closest we get to a small town, it seems to me, is Verona—and we know how that turned out: Verona was

Where civil blood makes civil hands unclean.

Again, biographers and critics have speculated for years concerning Shakespeare's feelings about his home town. Certainly he spent much more of his time in London than at home with his family in Stratford. After all, that's where his work was. As the very model of a provincial village, with its gossip and feuds and petty lawsuits, Stratford wouldn't have had much of a chance as a locale for the stories Shakespeare chose to dramatize. But the relative scarcity of references to small-town life is a bit puzzling.

The program in which I taught was housed in a small-town elementary school. Our large family of students, parents, and teachers made up a community within the school, which in turn was the nucleus of our area. Within our Options family, my class and Changeling formed a small, tighter family. Families within extended families within communities—a familiar pattern historically, though fairly uncommon now.

After ten years of Shakespeare, I was looking for a new way to challenge my students. Something that would take advantage of the skills and traditions that we had institutionalized, but also something more contemporary and more personal. As before, it had to be something serious, something substantial, something that could live up to the expectations that Shakespeare had nurtured within us. Thornton Wilder's *Our Town* seemed like the perfect answer.

Our Town, which won the Pulitzer prize for drama in 1938, is the first great modern American play, and the pre-eminent drama of American community life. The small town of Grovers Corners, New Hampshire, is a place we know by heart, and *Our Town* is justly famous for making it both a specific place in a specific time period and also a place that is universal and timeless. It was a huge hit on Broadway. The time was perfect for its two big themes: the love/hate feelings we have for the small towns that are the source of our most fundamental values, and our (related) inability to live in the present. Small-town America taught us loyalty, dignity, integrity, kindness, and the value of tradition. Yet it also showed us the narrowness, intolerance, and cultural limitations that sometimes went along with those values. In *Our Town,* the embodiment of these contradictions is the secretly alcoholic choir director, Simon Stimson. Everyone knows about his problems; some people are tolerant, some are cruel. Wilder's ability to give both sides equal weight, while making the outcome of their conflict inescapable, is one of the things that gives the play its remarkable power.

For my students—I was now teaching the 6th/7th/8th-grade class—*Our Town* was a significant departure from Shakespeare. At first, it seemed considerably easier and simpler. No odd or difficult words, no iambic pentameter, no complex rhetorical arguments or twisted, extended metaphors. After two or three readings, however, they began to see that it wasn't a simple play after all. In contrast to Shakespeare, nothing much happens. Instead of the peaks and valleys of dramatic tension that they were used to, there was a steady flow of common events—breakfast, gossip, school, courtship, choir practice, marriage—until the end. In the last act, all the tension and emotion that actors must work to restrain in the first two acts come out in one extraordinary moment. And it doesn't work unless the tone that Wilder demands has been sustained. The audience knows something is going to happen—there are several warnings from the Stage Manager—but the characters don't, and the tension between our knowledge and theirs is one of the key elements of the play. Accustomed to trying to get them to find and express the emotional components of their character's speech, now I had to remind them that (1) these people were New Englanders, stoic and taciturn by nature; and (2) it was the accumulation of tension that mattered. The impact of *Our Town* on its audience is a direct result of the actors' matter-of-fact reticence. What happens in the play is what usually happens in a small town, magnified by the weight it gathers as time passes and our knowledge and anxiety increase.

An important source of the play's appeal, and another departure from traditional theater, was the role of the Stage Manager. Sometimes he is simply a narrator. Then, suddenly, he crosses the line and becomes an actor in the play, or a commentator on the action. Is he supposed to be Wilder's alter ego? Is he God? Or possibly the audience's onstage agent, helping us through the story—a kind of dramatic travel guide? Whoever he is, he fits in perfectly with Wilder's other technical innovation: a bare set—ladders, a few tables, and the rest left to the audience's imagination. Before *Our Town*, a typical Broadway production was as grand and ornate as possible—set, costumes, lighting, everything. This was partly the influence of Hollywood: the biggest movie hits of the period were

Gone With the Wind and *The Wizard of Oz*. It was also a natural result of refinements in technical expertise, making more things possible onstage. In this context, the starkness of *Our Town* was shocking.

One of the more difficult stipulations of the script is the extensive and complicated pantomime required of some characters. Mrs. Gibbs, for example, has to light the fire, pump water into the kitchen sink, prepare breakfast, set the table, and make pie—all slowly and as realistically as possible, while conversing with her husband and children. Pantomime seems easy until you try it. Establishing an effective tempo and timing your actions to the dialogue is challenging—as is creating and remembering the space you're using. It was wonderful training for the actors, but it took hours of practice.

The hardest part of all, and what makes the play a challenge for student actors, is the last act. The curtain opens on three rows of chairs, facing the audience. Some are occupied, some are not—in such a way that we are able to see each person's face clearly. We recognize a few of the people from previous scenes, but they look different. Each person is calmly staring out over the heads of the audience. Not vacantly, but as though waiting, or listening for something. They seem incapable of surprise, yet also expectant. Not sad, simply resigned—and as if they know something that we do not yet know.

These are the dead, and the chairs are their grave markers. From their dialogue, it becomes apparent that they are soon to be joined by Emily Gibbs, who has recently died in childbirth, and whose funeral procession enters the cemetery as the dead finish their brief conversation. It's raining. Dressed in white, Emily suddenly appears from under the mourners' umbrellas. She seems confused, and slowly makes her way toward her grave. Before she can accept her death, she pleads with the Stage Manager for one last visit back in time, to a favorite day. The dead quietly urge her not to do this, but she insists, and chooses to relive her twelfth birthday. The Stage Manager agrees to let her try, and her family enters, gathering around the kitchen table and speaking to each other as they did on that day.

It doesn't work. Emily cannot bear it, and her famous cry from the heart is the climax of the play:

*I can't. I can't go on. It goes so fast. We don't have time to
look at one another. I didn't realize. So all that was going on
and we never noticed. Take me back—up the hill—to my
grave. But first: Wait! One more look. Good-bye. Good-bye,
world. Good-bye, Grover's Corners.... Mama, and Papa.
Good-bye to clocks ticking.... and Mama's sunflowers. And
food, and coffee. And new ironed dresses and hot baths....
and sleeping, and waking up. Oh, earth, you are too wonderful
for anybody to realize you!*

Getting this passage just right—making it believable—is very
difficult. For one thing, as an actress, you know you are expected to break
down, and knowing that makes reacting authentically harder (especially
after saying it dozens of times in rehearsal). Then there's the cumulative
pressure of the entire play, all that restrained built-up emotion, weigh-
ing on your small shoulders. For an actress to react credibly, she has to
completely give herself up, in a way that few younger teenagers are able
to do—which is why *Our Town* is rarely done below the high school level.

Of the six girls who played Emily in our two productions, five gave
credible and effective interpretations of these emotional words. The
sixth, a shy sixth-grader who previously had been reluctant to put herself
forward in any way, was the best friend of the girl (mentioned in the
last chapter) whose mother had recently died. Whether because of her
grief for her lifelong friend, or for other reasons, this student became
completely immersed in the role of Emily. As had happened in our
earliest *Hamlet* production, her quietly emotional passion in rehearsal
became a game-changer, forcing the older kids in class to take *Our Town*
seriously—to realize that the emotions called forth were real, that they
needed empathy instead of irony, and that the sooner they acknowledged
this, the better it would be for all of us.

In performance, S- was amazing. The soda fountain scene, where
Emily Webb and George Gibbs become unofficially engaged, was
perfectly understated. In the last act, when Emily sees the futility of
her effort to relive the past, S- was so completely transformed that,
instead of wiping her eyes when she started crying, she spoke through

her tears, totally in anguish. In all my years doing theater with young people, I had never seen this kind of complete identification with a character. In a trance, she slowly walked to her grave, and the last dry, understated lines of the play returned us to the timeless sleep of Grovers Corners.

After the performance, S- was helpless. For thirty minutes, she sat in the audience, still in costume, her father holding her as she sobbed uncontrollably. It was as if she had been possessed, and her parents were surprised and even a bit frightened by the intensity of her grief. S- was a very original writer, and a few months later, looking back at the play, she wrote this.

I remember
the night
that it happened,

When tears fell
through the sky
landing on magic.

When I was
chest deep in emotion
the feelings not reaching
my head.

When the clowns
were overflowing,
their faces a blur.

I remember
the night
when I felt it.

When my voice shook
and my feet
were an earthquake.

When the pressure
was lifted for
two hours
and I was free.

When my mind
was on overload,
so it gave up
completely.

I remember
the night
that it ended.

When my hands
and my eyes
were at war,
not wanting
the tears to fall.

When the arms
were around me
holding me up.

When the sadness
had no boundaries,
and the sobs
and the smiles
were endless.

Sometimes, it seemed as if we were doing a play for just one or two people in the cast, kids who for some reason had an almost desperate need for that particular play to be performed. I remember a production of *Much Ado About Nothing* that seemed guaranteed to fail—except that one student, whose alcoholic mother was making her home life miserable, was so determined that this one part of her life succeed, as a kind of compensation. During the first production of *Our Town*, a student who was new to our program, who had never before done theater, and who had her own family problems, completely wrapped herself up in the play—filling in for anyone who was gone, cueing people, coaxing people to memorize and helping them do so, making lists of props and pantomime segments and everything else. Seeing this, and watching the quiet intensity of S- as Emily, the other kids gradually got serious. And when they did, when they accepted the play for what it was—not Shakespeare, but something that had the potential to be emotionally powerful, if done right—*Our Town* came together.

It wasn't our best production, by any means. But for many students, it did open the doors of the moral imagination in a way that no previous play had done. Though set 100 years in the past, the world of Grovers Corners became concrete and accessible to them as a community like ours. They could easily imagine themselves as Howie Newsome on his paper route, or Joe Crowell delivering the milk, talking companionably to his horse. The girls who played the two mothers, Mrs. Gibbs and Mrs. Webb, found the characters' friendship and chore-sharing familiar, and the conversation between them was a very natural part of both productions. Because ours was a close-knit community, the mechanics and rituals of life in Grovers Corners, even the outdated ones, could be readily assumed. And the kids loved George's little sister Rebecca, who is equal parts innocent angel and annoying pest.

And as always, the complex web of relationships was their key to getting it right. The sixth-grader whose mother had recently died was much on their minds. She was playing an important role, but many days she was so sad that she couldn't practice. During the rehearsal period, there was a memorial service; six members of the cast decided to go, out of loyalty to their friend, so they could sing "Blest Be the Tie That Binds," Emily's favorite hymn and a vital element in the play. Counting on each other to sustain the serious tone of the play, and pulling it off, the actors were reinforced by the positive response of our community audience members; and in the end, many of them were surprised by how the message of the play became personally relevant.

It was my first time ever to cry while watching a play.

I remember my first rehearsal as Emily. At the end of the third act I didn't really feel what Emily feels. The words just spilled out of my mouth with very little emotion. In the last dress rehearsal I feel like I improved a whole lot. To me it was amazing, I have never played a character with so many feelings.

I will always remember the emotion we put into the words we spoke.

We went from a class who didn't want to do anything, to loving each other.

Support really helps to tie the bonds. Everyone supported me, and it meant so much to me!

I remember how everyone was nervous in their own way— being shy, being hyper, or just feeling it in your stomach.

It was really hard for me not to be really emotional, but after a lot of practice, I got it! That was the big change.

I changed my character by changing my point of view about life.

I thought a lot about how Mrs. Webb feels about her daughter, about seeing her only daughter die.

I will always remember in Sunflower Cast's dress rehearsal right after the big Emily speech, I sat back down in the graveyard and I looked over at A-, playing Mrs. Gibbs, and she was crying. And I looked at her and started crying.

The graveyard scene. So extremely powerful emotionally. Everyone goes, "Wait, this is real."

E- saying Emily's final words, and A- crying. And the long silences onstage.

The tie that binds. I will never (never!) forget our first performance, when we were so nervous (I was at least), and we pulled through and made a great play.

Never feeling like I could pull through and become Simon Stimson. Then leaving myself behind and jumping into Simon with every fiber of my being. I remember crying. And crying. Then crying some more. Becoming my character. Living, breathing, being Simon. Dying. Living. At first, just being angry as Simon. Then, being disturbed. And finally, being broken. Because that's what Simon was. Broken.

The last scene in the Sunflower Cast night performance, I looked out into the audience, and almost everyone was crying.

Being a mom (again), and having that awful feeling of losing someone.

I learned that I can do some really amazing things that I didn't know I could do. That I could bring Emily to life and actually put myself all the way into it.

[We learned] That people are blind. And that we need to think about what we do. And take time to look at things.…How people don't understand what they have until they lose it.… That it is kind of pointless unless you live life to the fullest.… That life is precious and sometimes sucks.… That life can be good and bad, it depends on how you live it – in fear, or living it the way you want to…That we only have a limited amount of life to live.

None of us are any more special than someone else. We're all going through life looking for the same thing. We all get yelled at by our mothers at breakfast. We all wonder if we're good-looking. We all find friends, and people we can rely on for life. And we all wish we would have done more in our life to live life to the fullest.

How important it is to spend time with the people you love while you still can. And how precious every minute of living is, and not to waste the precious time that you have.

That everything really isn't what it seems. When you look at Grovers Corners with blinders on it looks like a lovely town. When you take the blinders off, Simon shows the world that life isn't perfect. Life is so, so precious. You have to hold onto it, and love every, every moment of it.

Panic and mistakes are inevitable, trying to stop them is futile, and the best thing to do is just to "look only for what's ahead, and be ready for what's ahead." I learned that I can do some amazing stuff, so I don't always have to be so hard on myself. I learned that, when it comes to plays, I have a hard time letting go. After what I did with OT, I feel like I could play almost any part in the world. Drama has really given me a lot of confidence. It also helped me when I was in a bad mood, because I could become someone else and not have to worry for a while. At first, with Emily, I played her pretty well, I guess. But by the end, I had started not to play her, but to be her. I'll never, ever forget Emily. Never, ever, ever, ever.

I will always remember Emily in the third act. And in the drug-store, where my eyes picked up tears like clouds.

I mentioned the many differences between *Our Town* and Shakespeare, and they are substantial. The year *Our Town* was published, however, Thornton Wilder received a letter from a man in Princeton, New Jersey. The writer compared *Our Town* to *Hamlet*; he wrote, "That an American of the present day can create with such delicacy and detachment touches the soul like a miracle." The letter was signed, "A. Einstein, Mathematical Physicist."

The truths about human nature in Shakespeare are profound and timeless. Emily's revelation at the end of *Our Town* is intensely personal and emotional, but it had just as much of an impact on my students as Hamlet's dying words, and it was grounded in a more familiar and more concrete reality. Both visions are essential, and together they embody the fundamental goal of all theater, representing what Wilder called "the sense of what it means to be human."

Mrs. Gibbs and Emily. [*Our Town*]

photo by [C]hristine Castigliano

Leading with Your Heart

Our Town was a breakthrough for us, and also for me personally. It proved we could transfer what we had learned doing Shakespeare to something different, and succeed reasonably well. Previously stuck in my Shakespeare comfort zone, with *Our Town* I managed to step away and try something a little risky and uncertain. Ginger would have been proud! *Our Town* gave my students a new kind of learning experience. Here was a community like ours, with familiar comforts and problems. Taking advantage of the bonds that tied us together as a class, each student eventually found a place within that community; and through the universal story of what happened in Grovers Corners, they gained some insights about how they might lead their lives.

As well as being universal, the story is grounded in a richly detailed spatial and temporal context. We got to talk about how it was to live in small-town America during the early 1900s, what was the same (courtship rituals!—and ambivalence about marriage) and what was different (cars, phones, etc.). Thinking about Mrs. Gibbs hand-pumping water for the breakfast coffee, and Howie Newsome's horse-drawn milk wagon, made history a bit more concrete for my students—as did the many references to the social and political circumstances of the times. Mr. Webb, editor of the local paper, explains to the Stage Manager that *"All males vote at the age of twenty-one. Women vote indirect."* What do you suppose that means, I asked my class (after explaining the irony of the word "indirect"). And so we talked about Women's Suffrage—much surprise, and outrage that it took so long for women to win the right to vote.

Thinking over these various benefits after our performances, I went looking for a new play for us to try. I hoped it would be just as exciting and engaging as *Our Town*, with a similar historical dimension. Teaching middle schoolers, I needed something that would tie into my American History social studies curriculum, so I began searching for a period play that would be challenging, that would involve the kids in some social problem, and that had a suitable mix of male and female roles.

After a lot of effort, I decided that such a play didn't exist. While there were quite a few historical plays available, there simply were none with enough good roles for girls. Several plays about the Civil War looked great—but no female characters. I really like *Inherit the Wind*, about the Scopes Trial and the teaching of evolution, but again, it has only one female role worth mentioning.

I was very attracted to the 1930s as a good period for intensive study and dramatic possibilities. For one thing, the "recession" of 2008 (actually more like a mini-depression where we live) had just started to get serious, and I thought students would benefit from seeing what a previous period of economic uncertainty had been like. For another thing, I assumed that at least some of their grandparents would have lived through the 30s, and might be willing to share their experiences.

When I looked at possible plays about conditions in the 30s, however, I still couldn't find the right one. William Saroyan? I loved *The Time of Your Life*, but it was too long, and had only one female role. Clifford Odets? *Waiting for Lefty* is justly famous for embodying the labor struggle, but again, few female roles. Horace McCoy's *They Shoot Horses, Don't They* is brilliant, but overwhelmingly depressing. And so on.

Finally, not knowing what else to do, I decided to write my own play. I had no experience, but I knew the period well and I knew my students. I would write something about families who were struggling economically, and how they coped with it. With few expectations, I sat down on my backyard patio one summer morning and started to write. Two weeks later, I had something I thought we could use. I decided on a pseudonym so I could be anonymous, and entitled the play *Hard Times*.

It's 1935. Their farms foreclosed, the Nolan and Martin families have recently moved into a tenement house in Cleveland. Jobs are hard to find, and Sarah Nolan's husband Thomas has gone on the road looking for work. Every morning, Elizabeth Martin and the kids make bread and turnovers to sell to local shops. Both families eagerly await Thomas's letters, always hoping for good news.

Out on the road, Thomas meets hoboes, tramps, runaways, political exiles, and dozens of unemployed men like himself, all struggling to find a decent job and keep their self-respect. Around the campfires at night, he hears their stories and shares his own, making the kind of connections that become a substitute for family, and that keep people going in difficult circumstances.

Other people live in the tenement house, and their stories also reflect the hard choices required of ordinary people by the Great Depression. Daniel Stuart is an idealistic reporter for the *Cleveland Plain Dealer.* Miranda Alessandro runs her own beauty shop. Aunt Jessie is a librarian. Mrs. Dailey works as a seamstress, and Mr. Moseley drives a trolley car.

Of course, it's impossible to tell the story of an entire era in only two hours. Many important things had to be left out—such large-scale events as the Bonus March, hunger riots, and the dust bowl migrations, for example. On the other hand, history is also about individual people and families, their experiences, what they shared, and the conflicts among them. It's about strong feelings, our shared emotional responses to change. *Hard Times* is a collection of snapshots from one of many Great Depression family albums. Obviously, I hoped the pictures would tell a larger story, because these are not the only people who faced these particular problems and conflicts. The play is a gallery, then, of examples—the varieties of that daily struggle against seemingly strange and mysterious forces that drove ordinary people to try sometimes desperate things. And in that trying, to find ways of working together and helping each other.

In *Hard Times,* as in real life, the struggles began with people making the hard choices dictated by necessity. Thomas's decision to leave his family and look for work on the road west was a common one: at the height of the Depression, 25 percent of Americans were unemployed. There were only so many street corners on which to sell apples or shine shoes. Necessary it may have been, but his decision ripped apart the social fabric, and made life harder for everyone at home. Kelly and Maggie, his teenage daughters, want to help out so badly that they decide to do something really risky—bringing about more conflict. Mrs. Dailey and the women she works with feel compelled to stop work one day, to protest impossible working conditions—taking a risk that their boss would simply fire them. Daniel's printers go out on strike, and he has to decide whether to honor his principles and the picket line, or betray them and keep his job. Miranda has several tough choices to make: should she help Kelly and Maggie get the jobs they want, and should she join her life with Daniel's, with all its uncertainties.

The responses to these choices, the conflicts they create, and the effect of those conflicts on the extended family at the center of the story: that's the basic plot. To understand the context of those choices, though, required a lot of background preparation. My students (and, I suspect, most middle-school students) knew almost nothing about the 1930s, other than the fact that the stock market crashed. To make the decade more real to them, we did several play-related projects. We watched two excellent documentaries, one on the Dust Bowl, another that featured in-depth interviews with people who had been on the road during that time, either as hoboes or as migrant workers. I handed out several relevant interviews from Studs Terkel's classic oral history, also called *Hard Times*. And we read the chapters on the 1930s in Howard Zinn's *A Young People's History of the United States.*

The best project, the one that really personalized the period for them, was a radio interview assignment. I asked them to research, in pairs, the experiences of a real-life counterpart of someone in the play—a hobo, a journalist, a hairdresser, a taxi dancer, and so on. Each team was to prepare a question-and-answer interview for taping on a simulated 1930s radio show. The kids liked this project a lot. They acted out the interviews, and I made an audio tape. Here's a sample:

> Q: What was your life like before you started working at the dance hall?
> A: My life was really hard, and that's the only reason I started working there. My family didn't agree with me working at the dance hall, but it was the only way I could help put food on the table.

Q: Was there a lot of competition? How did the other dancers treat you?

A: There was a lot of competition, because they were all looking for money, just like me. The other dancers didn't treat me with any respect. They would steal my make-up or "accidentally" spill food on my dress, and other mean things. But I just had to ignore it.

Q: Did people treat you differently after they found out you worked there?

A: People did treat me differently. Everyone at school called me a slut, but I learned to ignore it because I knew it wasn't true. My family wouldn't talk to me for a while, they were still angry at me for getting a job without asking them first. One time my dad came into the dance hall and saw how I was acting around the guys and was very disappointed in me.

Q: Would you recommend this job to other teenage girls who need the money?

A: If they were tough I would say go ahead, but be careful. If they weren't, then no, try to find some other job.

The casts of both productions of *Hard Times* were enthusiastic about the play from the beginning. Because the roles had been written to fit individual students, the characters were more of a natural fit than in other plays, closer to the students' own ages and sharing many of their own concerns about autonomy, dependence, and possible futures. Better still, the story was centered around several connected families, making use of the strong bonds within our class and program family. In addition, we inserted a prologue that featured swing dancing (learned by many of them just for the play) and a game of Monopoly (invented in the 30s) on the front porch. This made the transition into the first scene really easy, for both cast and audience. And there was swing dancing in the aisles at intermission—several grandparents joining in! There was lots of other music—the hoboes sang Woody Guthrie songs and IWW anthems around the campfire, and the younger kids in the tenement house serenaded Thomas's wife with the couple's favorite song, "You Are My Sunshine." There was gentle sibling teasing, and some really awful jokes. There was anxiety, but it was bounded by the reassurance of a close-knit family.

As previously mentioned, there was also conflict. One of the things I tried to do in the play was to give my students a safe place to try out strong feelings—which adolescents sometimes get few opportunities to do. The main conflict in the play causes an extended argument between Daniel and Miranda, both of whom are defending basic values. Other characters yearn to be reunited with a parent, or to be grown up and taken seriously. I hoped that going through these situations vicariously would be good practice for them. After all, this is one of the things theater does best, as indicated by many of our survey responses. The conflicts in the play are intense, but all of them are talked out, and I hoped this would be a good experience also, showing the students that conflict itself is not a tragedy, and that you could stand up for yourself and still figure out a way to get along with others.

In the end, *Hard Times* proved to be an effective way of teaching the 1930s. My students were impressed with how widespread the suffering was, and many of them gained a new appreciation of their own good fortune at not having to go through it. The play also made them realize how important it was to be connected with others who were struggling. And after singing "Union Maid" together so many times, they had a better chance of remembering the meaning of the word "solidarity."

> *I had no idea how hard the Great Depression was until I did this play. I learned how desperate people were.*

> *I learned that there were these places hoboes lived in called "Hoovervilles," named after President Hoover.*

> *The hoboes made up their own code about whether an area was safe or not. Some hoboes left their families for adventure, too.*

> *It was hard to leave your family. Girl hoboes had it really hard.*

Life can't always go the way you planned, especially in hard times. People had to deal with the dust, and no jobs, not much money, and not the greatest health. People had to deal with leaving their families and their homes.

I didn't know how hard it was for people just to get food for their kids. I'll never see it the same way again.

A lot of people had to fight tooth and nail for food and jobs. Many kids went for the life of the hobo, to lighten the family bills—and to see the country. Riding the rails became like a subculture for many folk. For some, it was all they had. No homes or family, only the rails. With a sliding metal door for a window and door, wood, steel, or iron as flooring, only one room to share among all, and a whole country for a yard, it could be a hard life.

Families were brought closer, and torn apart. Risks were taken. People were literally scratching and scraping for every penny. Family was all you had sometimes, and for some, they didn't even get that. So you made a new one.

I learned about what hard times are really like. The 1930s was a time that was extra hard, and I think I caught a glimpse of what it felt like to grow up in a time like that.

Before, I knew minimal information about the Depression, no details. This play taught me 85-90% of what I know about the 1930s.

The 30s made such a big impact on so many people. It's just amazing that we got to feel the least little bit of what they felt. We're saying, this is what was. This is what could be. And this is what we need to do to get through it.

The people in the play taught me that when something goes wrong, it's best to stick together, and never give up.

Daniel taught me that sometimes life doesn't work out the way you want. Aunt Jessie taught me not to give up.

Life isn't always easy! Especially in hard times like these. But family is always there for you. Even if they have to leave. They are always inside of you.

They taught me to keep your family close, because when they're gone you'll want them again. People all have sides you've never seen, and when a light is shined on them, well then that's amazing, and that happened in this play!

Never give up, and do what you have to for the ones you love.

Be grateful for what you have now, because you may not have it in the future. And listen to your friends and family, they have important things to say.

Mrs. Dailey taught me to not try to be that perfect angel. Thomas taught me not to give up, even when the only thing keeping you walking is the chance you might be home for Christmas. Miranda taught me to stand up for myself. And John taught me to stay on that road, from something bad to something better.

I am convinced that the effectiveness of the play for teaching history was strengthened by the fact that it provoked some of the strongest actor-character identifications yet. Did the circumstances of the characters' lives create a sense of sympathy that made the bonds stronger? Perhaps, or maybe it was the closeness and support of the extended family in the play, the way they all pitched in together to survive. Surely in some way this was every student's unconscious hope for her own family situation. For whatever combination of reasons, the people of *Hard Times* were taken totally to heart by my actors.

I remember everyone who was in the play, and how much I care for them. Having the amazing chance to bring someone to life who has an important story to tell. Performing in front of what seems to be a million people watching every move you make. Whenever I set foot onstage during rehearsal and performances I always felt my inner old lady [she played Mrs. Dailey, the seamstress] *come out and be a part of everyone's lives, especially Kate's.*

I will always remember the adrenaline rush of stepping on the stage, how blank my head would feel and how I would just forget myself and only know truly how my character felt and how she thought.

People got so into their characters. The delivery of every line, the constant reviewing of the scenes with each other before we went on, the energy and passion that everyone brought to the stage.

I love the parts of the play where all the hoboes are talking. They are always about some kind of storytelling and people getting along, even though it is hard to trust someone you just met, but they somehow end up doing just that. I really love the boxcar story, because it just really proves how bad it was then and how desperate people were.

[The "boxcar story" from *Hard Times:*

HOBO 1: I was in a boxcar with some pretty desperate characters one time, traveling on the SP in Texas somewhere. They were pretty cockeyed already when I got on, so I stayed off in a corner with my partner. We were gonna get some shuteye, but these gentlemen started yelling about who had the last hit at the bottle, then one of 'em pushed the other one down and said, what the hell, I got something even better than this crap. Then he pulled out a can of sterno & a can opener, opened it up. Dug around in his pockets & found a sock or something, then he strained the sterno through the sock, right into his mouth. He was roarin' & cussin' something fierce for a few minutes after that, then he just fell out & went off to the Land of Nod. I didn't hear a peep out of him the whole rest of the trip. When we jumped off in east Texas his buddy was kicking at him, tryin' to wake him up before the bulls showed up.]

My favorite part of the play was the drunk scene with Maggie and Kelly and the guys from the dance hall, when Daniel comes out with his "gun" and saves them. It's my favorite scene because you really get to see Daniel and Miranda connect with each other, in a way that is rare.

[Daniel and Miranda, from *Hard Times:*

Miranda: Now you're...different. The way you talked to Kevin. You're leading with your heart, now. That's a hard step to take, especially in hard times like these. A lot of people freeze up, act tough, get tough. Or pretend to be.
Daniel: That's funny...myself, I feel stronger now. Maybe softer on the outside, stronger on the inside...Thanks to you, and Jessie, and those kids. Seems like before, it was all talk.]

My favorite lines were Miranda's long speech in the fight scene between Daniel and her, when T- said it she really sounded like Miranda, and I always got so caught up in what she was saying that I teared up a little.

One of my favorite places was the next to last scene, when Miranda is cutting Kevin's hair and they start talking about Miranda making Kevin look like a dog, and they get into this whole conversation about it and at the end Kelly says, "This conversation is going to the dogs," and I laughed every time.

This play really changed the way I look at things sometimes, especially the way things are now. It makes me think a lot harder about people and all the hard things they go through to get what they need. It has changed the viewpoint of many people, including me!

Having the feeling Sarah had with her husband gone, that feeling of a mix between maybe sad, angry, scared for the family—those feelings will really stick with me, and that's not a bad thing. I KNOW it definitely made Sarah much stronger on the inside.

I thought at first my character was just a tough guy, but thanks to the drama exercises we did I thought more about him. Now I think he's a good friend, too.

At first I thought Liz Martin was just some random old lady. But once we started blocking, she really came to life. I thought Miranda and Kelly were both very annoying. Miranda was way too bossy, and Kelly was just irritating. I can't quite explain it, but as we got farther into the play, all the differences didn't seem to matter so much.

Instead of thinking, I just did what I thought John and the hobo would say and do.

I kept adding more emotion and more gestures. I began to get a better idea about how difficult the Great Depression was by reading books and watching films. With the costume, and the realistic set, I began to get a feeling that I actually was Kevin Martin in a 1930s tenement house, and that I was looking for a job. Performances were even better.

I actually felt like it really WAS hard times. And I really felt I knew how it was, after doing the play. I kinda had a new understanding about some things, too, like Life can't always go the way you planned. Sometimes one of your family might have to leave to help the family. Hopefully things will get better.

Miranda wasn't just some girl who dropped out of high school and worked in a beauty shop, she was a girl who had some hard times during the Great Depression. She wanted the best for Maggie, Kelly, Jessie, and everyone in the tenement. She wanted people to realize that there was more to the world than what they saw and I think, in the end, she ended up seeing that as well. Sarah Nolan, hmmm, last minute changes. She wanted Thomas home to lay down the law with Maggie and Kelly, but she also wanted her husband home. She ended up more forceful and I think that's good. She kinda came to life before my eyes. I really felt like I was being told what to do by her. And at first she was reluctant and didn't want to do the play, it seemed too fake. But it became real. And Kate, she listened, and stood up when she was excited, and has a path, maybe somewhere different from what she and Mrs. Dailey thought, but she'll find it. She's taking the world one step at a time, but Prince Charming is coming.

Making my characters more slow and thoughtful helped. Putting in pauses made them sound more human—they didn't KNOW what they were going to say. Just internalizing my character in general gave me more emotion to work with.

I got to be a little girl again. And I got to be 16. I got to be a librarian. I got to be many people. The people I worked with were incredible.

I really thought the play was exciting and fun, and I really liked being who I was, because I got to play an old lady, then young girls, so I got different perspectives.

My characters are internalized, there's no way they're getting out. I'm a new person. Sarah Nolan and I are still waiting. Thomas came home, but now he's gone again, so we're still waiting for that day. Daniel and Miranda, well they've seen both sides of the story, but we don't know where they'll end up. Miranda's not gonna let anyone talk her or her opinion down, and I'm learning. This play opened my eyes quite a bit, about a lot of things. And I think our class is more of a family now. Yeah, I feel bigger inside, but I also feel like I know everyone around me better.

Thinking about the lines, for example the last letter. As Mrs. Dailey, Emily, or Kate, thinking of those words: "Some day soon you're gonna be sitting out on the porch, and you're gonna hear somebody yell your names, and it'll be me, coming home. Right now my old arms are aching for wantin' to hug you all. I can't do that, so you all have to hug each other for me. But it won't be long."

The first class to do this play, in 2009, was an unusual group. Quite a few of the students were very bright intellectually, others were creative in different areas. As always, some had come from other schools and were lost for a while. What stood out, in the beginning, was how difficult it was for them to stop criticizing each other—and themselves. High expectations were one thing, but public correction of others is poisonous to all. Having two sets of siblings (one set was twins) in the class didn't help, nor did the fact that several families were coming apart during the school year.

Our Town helped this group become more functional, but after *Hard Times* it was hard to believe they were the same group. I think many of their comments reflect a huge sense of relief, as they sensed the difference the play made—for them as individuals, and as a group.

I will always remember how well we did. And how we went from pretty low to really high. How our first per-formance went. I really love this play.

I remember learning all the songs. And the performances seemed so unreal. En - trance. And how it seemed like a replay of Our Town in so many ways, and yet not at all. It all seemed so far off and long ago, but kind of like yes-terday, like we were really living those days all over again, like Emily in Our Town, going back.

I will never forget how spoiled I am. I get mostly everything, while the people in the Depression didn't. I will never forget this play.

Learning how to dance. Hanging out with my friends. Singing the hobo songs backstage. I made a lot of discoveries about myself this year. I saw a lot of things I never noticed were there. I feel so oblivious for never noticing!

Unforgettable: being Emily, seeing A- read the last part of the letter: "Your husband, father, and uncle, Thomas Nolan." The class laughing with each other, happy, singing "Union Maid" and "Pastures of Plenty" and "Hobo's Lullaby" backstage. The looks in my classmates' eyes at the end of the last performance. Some crying in sadness. Some screaming with joy. And some thinking, this play is so great, I can never leave it.

In the end it wasn't fair for it to be over so soon. We only had the set up for three days but somehow in the end it felt like home. They were taking it down and it was like, "What are you doing?" but you couldn't say that because they wouldn't understand. They just wanted to get back to their own lives. They would say something stupid like, "You need to get home." "But THIS is my home, you're taking my life!" "It's okay, it's been two hours, it's over." But it's not. It doesn't end there. You see as much of it as you want to see.

I will never forget this play. One of the big things is being onstage as your character and interacting with other people. Also, singing the songs, onstage and off, that helped a lot. But the GIANT thing was hearing the last sentence of Thomas's letter at the end, and bowing. This was my best play yet.

The smell of my hair-spray, and of Mrs. Dailey's make-up, and the smell of the "bread dough." I love that feeling

when you walk out of the school, when you just did some-
thing really amazing. The cold air in your lungs, the smell
of the pine trees and the lake, the taste of the cool air, the
love that went into it, all the emotion.

After doing Hard Times, I feel an embarrassing sense of
relief. Because, well, playing Miranda was quite a dragon-
slaying battle for me. But what I mainly feel is a large
amount of pride. I'm so proud of everyone (including my-
self), because Hard Times is an important story to tell and
everyone did a MARVELOUS job!!

Three years later, we did the play again, and two of the original cast
returned to reprise the roles they had played in 2009. One of these was
a wonderful young actor whose life, during the three-year interim, had
turned upside down: he had suffered some serious health problems, he
had dropped out of high school and started home-schooling, his parents
had lost their jobs, and the family had been homeless for a time. In spite
of all this—and because his parents were so supportive—this young
man had proven to be one of the most positive and resilient students I
have ever known. He was thrilled to be acting in *Hard Times* again, and
because of his long experience with Changeling, I talked him into being
my assistant director.

Home-schooling is like taking a hike through a foggy
forest. It can be tiring, it can be lonely; infinitely more
worth while than running on exercise equipment at a gym,
but lonely and foggy nonetheless. The Hard Times
rehearsals broke up that fog. Having the opportunity to
spend time with old friends, to make new ones, and even
just enjoy the sound of another human voice—the time
spent back at Options was incredible. Having a chance to
play at being a director in one room, and forcing L-, B-, and
K- to redo the same scene over and over again, getting my
face painted, and playing Guardian Angel just like we used
to: when I went to Bob's class, all of these things are memo-
ries that I'll be holding onto for a good long while.

I had begun to think that the stage-play part of my life was over. I went to high school, I wasn't planning on drama club, I had no idea that I would once again be part of an Options production. I should have guessed they would never let me go. So over the course of a few weeks I found out I'd be performing as a hobo, and a few weeks later I found out that I'd be performing as Daniel. A few weeks later I was onstage, breathing heavily and feeling as if my bowels planned on forcing their way out of my stomach. It was just like old times.

It's impossible to truly describe what it's like to be backstage, whispering with your comrades, nervous exhilaration rising in your throats as you realize that at any time you could be onstage, that the play you've put your soul into is ACTUALLY HAPPENING, and you breathe heavily, you start panting, and...it works. Somehow, the play happens, and you realize you can do this, and you just start to get into your role, and you're picking up steam and...the play's over. Before you realize it, you've hit the end. The last performance is finished. YOU'RE finished. And you don't know how it happened, but you know one thing, the last few days were incredible. They were a blur, but you can say with certainty that those days weren't wasted. In the last few days you became something, someone, and you can't wait to get onstage again.

No part of this play can come close to the fight scene for me. Being able to let go, to really rage, to say the things you've been wanting to say, and to get slapped for saying them, to realize that maybe you were wrong, and maybe, just maybe you had completely ignored what was in front of you the whole time, it creates tension, and you can feel Daniel transform. He stops being a sap and becomes a person. A person you could get to like. That scene holds the magic for me.

Doing this play made me realize something: I'm an actor. Maybe I'm a scientist, a writer, a five-star therapist, but

I'm an actor too. And it's not something I plan on giving up any time soon.

The first time I did this play, I was younger, more naive, more ready to accept the characters of the play at face value. This time around, I found this casual acceptance of the characters more difficult. More specifically, I had trouble accepting MY character. I found Daniel...annoying. Like a boy scout, all words and "cub honor" and no action, no depth. But performing this play, I felt Daniel transform, become someone I could relate to, someone I admired. Watching Daniel change changed me, and gave me something to aspire to. And being back, it was great. Like Daniel said, "I'll be carrying you guys around with me the rest of my life."

As adolescents, my students were learning to see themselves in some kind of larger framework, as part of something bigger. Like all of us, they were looking for some kind of larger meaning in the events of their lives. The people in *Hard Times* do that, too. Like us, they hope to justify the choices they make—often, the choices they are forced to make. Sometimes, that means doing something pretty hard, even scary, like what Maggie and Kelly did. Sometimes, hard times did involve choosing between saving your honor and feeding your kids.

For most of the people in the play, connecting with others became their lifeline. *"But we gotta help, Ma. We gotta keep the family afloat, or we'll all sink."* The metaphor is well-used, but the sentiment is what probably saved us, as families and as a nation on the edge of disaster in the 1930s. The history of the Great Depression is a history of pain and deprivation, but it is also a history of discovery; and one of the things Americans discovered (or rediscovered) was family. World War I and the 1920s were hard on community in this country. It took a disaster to wake us up to what is really important.

Every play we did was a bit like that, too. For a long time, it was hard to figure out how we were going to take the risks that would make it happen. Gradually, because our family was there for us, we came to believe—in the play, in the cast, in ourselves.

Tina and Marty. [*Bring the War Home*]

Emily and Kate [*Hard Times*]

Blood Will Have Blood

Inspired by *Hard Times*, when the summer rolled around again I decided to write another play, and the subject was never in doubt. When you teach middle-school American History, it helps to find themes and time periods that will be interesting, that connect to contemporary issues in some way, and that bring together as many currents of past history as possible. If you can also hit upon a subject that has been neglected, such as the history of ordinary people in the 1930s, that's even better, because it usually means that students will not have preconceived ideas about "what really happened."

For me, the Vietnam War era was the perfect choice. The 1960s is generally regarded by scholars as one of the three most exciting decades in our past (the others are the 1860s and the 1930s). So many things happened, and so many cultural changes began to take place. The term "watershed" is another overused metaphor, but it fits. In fact, a recent Oregon Shakespeare Festival play about the 60s was called *Continental Divide*.

I wasn't interested in showing the actual violence of combat in the play, that has been done in the movies and onstage many times. What has been badly neglected is the conflict within the "hearts and minds" of ordinary people—and especially, those in the peace movement. Much has been written about the battles, the tactics, and the soldiers—and not so much on the experiences of those who played a huge part in finally bringing the war to an end. The stereotypical "hippie peace freak" of TV and the movies is just that, a stereotype. Yet he or she bears the dubious burden of representing everyone who was ambivalent about the killing, or who thought the war could never be won and therefore should end, or who thought ALL wars were wrong, or who just wished our country would mind its own business—or anyone who wasn't gung-ho in favor of continuing the war. Much more interesting, to me, was the critical and ongoing conflict within the peace movement itself about how best to try and stop the fighting in Southeast Asia. The movement was diverse, and even splintered; and every group had a different idea about tactics—and especially, about the role of violence.

I was a minor participant in the peace movement for several years, and I remember the constant struggle over this issue. Was violence ever acceptable? Only to property? To what extent could one ethically defend oneself and others from the violence of the authorities? Was pacifism a basic principle, or just the correct tactic? Was Gandhi's way the only moral way, or did it not really apply outside of the context in which he created it? Were all wars bad, or just this one? Was there ever any such thing as a "just" war, and how do you decide? These were never simply abstract questions. For one thing, you had to know the answers before every demonstration, because they were unpredictable. For another thing, if you were eligible to be drafted, and decided to call yourself a conscientious objector, you were sure to be cross-examined along these lines by your local draft board. And what if you went to basic training, were sent to Vietnam, and only then realized you couldn't kill—what happened then?

I decided to make this conflict the central theme of the play. Not in order to give a "right" answer—many people in the movement went back and forth on these questions for years, especially after the killings at Kent State and Jackson State in May of 1970—but to explore how the conflict between competing answers made the war real to ordinary Americans, how it brought the war home.

Hoping that few students would notice the rather transparent parallels with *Hard Times* (if you're going to be a formula writer, use a formula that's been proven to work!), once again I started with several families sharing the same house, a large rooming house called Rivendell in the university district of a big city. As in *Hard Times*, they are struggling against a common enemy—in this case, the war. And as in *Hard Times,* deciding how to fight the common enemy brings conflict into an extended family. The late 60s/early 70s period was not the 1930s, however, and *Bring the War Home* is different in several important ways. The dangers are more threatening, more physical, more sinister. Poverty and hunger are often desperate situations, but solidarity can pull you through—the message of *Hard Times.* Solidarity is not as effective against tear gas and enemy bullets. The small-town innocence and traditional values that grounded people struggling in the Depression weren't nearly as useful in the late 1960s. The people who live at Rivendell came there from domestic trauma and foreign battle zones. They have experienced and witnessed things no foreclosed farmer could even dream about. That was the context I hoped to establish for my story. And because it was set in a time period through which I lived, and of which I still have many intense memories, the play more or less wrote itself. I finished it in a week. The basic story was fairly simple—here's my synopsis, from the program notes:

By 1971, the peace movement had been through many changes. Seven years of United States involvement in the Vietnam War had exhausted some, confused many, crystallized great numbers into resistance, and embittered a few to the point of considering—and actually using—violence. In many places, especially college campuses, the war and resistance to it had become the central focus of daily life.

Just off Southwest Broadway in Portland, Oregon, several families find themselves sharing an old rooming house called Rivendell. Magpie Rogers and her three kids have lived there a while, but Isis Lawrence and her daughters have just recently arrived from Berkeley. Vietnam vet Dennis Swantner (known as Denizen), editor of the local underground paper, and his younger brother Maxwell also live at Rivendell, as do Caroline and her mom Tina Blumenthal—a nurse who is another Vietnam vet.

As the story opens, the Lawrence family is trying to start over after something traumatic (we never learn exactly what) happened to them in Berkeley. All three are strong people, and 17-year-old Lorelei and 14-year-old Syrene were both politically involved in Berkeley. But their resilience is about to be tested by the events of the next few weeks.

As the younger kids in the house prepare for an upcoming demonstration, Denizen and his brother are moving toward a show-down over tactics, and friends begin to take sides. The war invades Tina's heart, Maxwell's body, and the streets around Rivendell. Like the actual "peace" that eventually ended the war itself, the peace at the end of *Bring the War Home* is ambiguous at best.

Writing this play was easier than writing *Hard Times*, and I had fun building the characters from 60s friends, acquaintances, and street legends—as well as from an imagination fueled by years of reading about that era. Missing Shakespeare a little, I not only gave Denizen a copy of the *Complete Works* to read obsessively in his wheel chair, but also allowed him to quote liberally and oracularly from it in his conversations. Some 60s folks didn't leave home without their battered copy of the *I Ching;* for Dennis, Shakespeare was the equivalent. Tina and Marty Blumenthal, the combat nurses, owed some of their hard-bitten competence to the years I spent watching the only TV show I ever watched compulsively, *MASH*. David Kirby's grand entrance and crazy antics in the first scene were stolen from Murray Burns's shenanigans in *A Thousand Clowns*—thanks, Herb Gardner. And so on. Naturally, I never admitted any of this to my students, who believed (for quite a long time) that *Bring the War Home*, like *Hard Times*, had been written by a mysterious playwright named Sydney Lawson. I definitely did not want to be part of the discussions about the plays, so a pseudonym seemed appropriate. When someone kept after me about why Sydney had no Wikipedia entry, and didn't show up on internet searches…I finally confessed. Fortunately, that didn't happen until after both plays had been produced.

As with *Hard Times*, we did lots of classroom work that integrated the play into our regular curriculum. The material on the war itself is overwhelming; I tried to find documentaries that were concise, fair, and aimed at middle-schoolers. I avoided war movies entirely, for many reasons. The popular music of the late 60s/early 70s was a perfect entry point for my students, and I used the lyrics to begin many conversations about cultural changes, and to jump-start writing projects. The kids did research projects on a wide range of topics—Bob Dylan, fashion trends, the Civil Rights Movement, student activism, and so on. As before, our basic text was the relevant material from the second volume of Zinn's *Young People's History*, and the excellent website that supports it.

Reaching out to veterans' groups, I was able to connect with two nurses who had been in Vietnam during the war. Both visited the classroom and gave presentations, and we had two extended discussions about their experiences, with many questions from the students. One of the nurses brought along a friend who was a combat veteran. She warned me beforehand that he had never been willing to say much about the circumstances of his service, and was probably not going to speak in class. Whether because a group of younger teenagers posed no threat to him, or because he saw that they were genuinely interested in learning about it, after her talk he made a comment, then gradually opened up and—with many pauses—gave a general account of his experiences, and answered some questions. Several groups of vets, including the nurses, ended up attending the performances. The combat vet who visited us came back to see the play a second time, and my nurse contact reported that he was impressed and pleased with what he saw.

One scene was difficult for him, and the nurse said he was crying during it. This was a scene with the Free Clinic (where Tina is the nurse) on one side of the stage, and her sister Marty's nursing station in Vietnam on the other side. Lit by a soft spotlight, Marty sits writing the letter that Tina (similarly lit) is reading aloud.

Dear Sis,

I hope you can read this. My hands are shaking so badly I can barely hold the pen. I am so wiped out I barely remember my name. God how I wish I could talk to you directly, hear your voice actually say my name, because I lost myself a little bit today and I am still kinda finding my way back.........don't worry I'm really okay but this has really really been a horrible week.

Things are falling apart here. I didn't want to tell you last time, and I still worry that you're gonna freak out. But I have to tell somebody about this stuff or I'll lose it completely and run screaming out into the jungle.

We just worked three hours trying to save this kid who had been shot in the neck. Two weeks ago we would have saved him. Not this time. We ran *out of plasma. Can you imagine what that's like? Maybe you can, maybe that happened to you over here, but somehow I think you would have said so…to work so hard, for so long, to almost make it over the hump, to see his vitals come up, and then…not be able to save him because we ran out of blood…We had a guy on the phone the entire three hours, trying and trying to find some more. Nobody would let go, just another sign of how supremely f****d-up everything has become here. He died. On the table. 19 years old. From Ohio. Dwayne. I memorized his face. I'll never, ever forget him. He's it, for me—I'm getting out.*

Don't worry, I'm not going over the fence. I just mean, I'm putting in for a CO. I just cannot believe this is the right thing to do any more.

No antibiotics a lot of the time. Always low on plasma. Equipment falling apart. Choppers falling out of the sky from no maintenance. Half my orderlies AWOL or on drugs. Food shortages—food! Somebody's making a huge killing on the black market here. Morale completely in the toilet—have you heard about fragging yet—our own guys throwing grenades into the tents of officers who send them out on patrol. Jeez God.

And then there's Agent Orange. Defoliant, supposed to make it easier to win the war…it takes the leaves off the trees all right. It also takes the skin off people's arms and legs. And the native population is starting to report horrible birth defects, probably from this stuff, since it's been around about a year now. What a nightmare.

So, the good news is, I'm out of here. As soon as I can file & get it processed. And that's not the horror of today's experience speaking, that's a promise. Sure, I'll keep doing my job, probably be a month or so before I walk. But I'm free.

Sorry for so much gruesome detail, Sis. It helped me, like you always have. More soon. You might be hearing from the Army, about my CO thing. Tell them anything, just help me get out of here.

Big hugs to all, especially The Kid.

Love forever, Marty

I learned so many things from reading and watching Shakespeare's plays. One of the most useful was, "show, don't tell." At the end of *The Winter's Tale*, when Paulina shows Leontes the newly-made wax "statue" of his wife—whom he believes long dead—Hermione's face looks so real that he expresses a desire to kiss her. Paulina's answer—

> *Good my lord, forbear:*
> *The ruddiness upon her lip is wet;*
> *You'll mar it if you kiss it, stain your own*
> *With oily painting.*

gives us a direct physical sense of the moment. In *MND*, Hermia's father catalogs Lysander's gifts to her, to prove how infatuated he is: *"bracelets of thy hair, rings, gawds, conceits, / knacks, trifles, nosegays, sweetmeats."* And of course, for physicality, nothing trumps Hamlet's shocker to his mother when he drags off Polonius's body—*"I'll lug the guts into the neighbor room."* These are only a few of the infinite number of strong, physical images in Shakespeare. It was a wise critic who wrote—oversimplifying, of course—that Shakespeare's plays are mostly about "food, sex, and death." These images are what made his people and his stories real to his audience—the "groundlings" who paid a penny to stand and watch in front of his stage for two hours were notoriously impatient with abstract speeches.

I tried hard not to make *Bring the War Home* a play about issues. Anything you can say about the politics of the war is bound to make someone defensive, and what I really wanted to do was show the students and the audience how it felt—how it felt to be caught up in the madness of war, and how it felt to try and resist it. This is what theater does: "what it is to be human" (Thornton Wilder) is to have strong feelings, to be personally and sensorily involved in life. Marty's letter, and Tina's reactions—her tears and anger—turned abstract horror into physical images and personal feelings, or so I hoped. War and resistance proceed from issues and ideas, but these are not nearly as real to young people as Marty's personal experience of trying to save a dying soldier.

As a result, I put in lots of stage business: people selling newspapers and candles on the street, dancing, reading Tarot cards, a big demonstration, an emergency operation, etc. The war and the conflicts it generated were part of our daily lives. While they wondered and brainstormed and argued about what to do, the people in the play were doing all these ordinary things. And talking about Bob Dylan songs and *The Lord of the Rings* and the new Beatles movie while they did them. And dancing and listening to "Green Onions," "Fortunate Son" (the GIs' favorite song in Vietnam), "All Along the Watchtower," and all the other great hits that make up the sound track for the play.

Even more so than *Hard Times, Bring the War Home* proved to be intensely emotional for the actors. And the sense of having given life to the people within its story seemed quite satisfying.

> *Strong emotions coming out. Transformations. Tears.*
> *Faces in the audience concentrating and glowing with*
> *joy. The excitement after the show. The compliments*
> *during the circle when it was over. Feeling the power of*
> *the words, and the emotions of the characters. The magic*
> *of spending four months of hard work, with the pain of*
> *separating from your character.*

> *Tina having the flashback. Kirby talking to Mike Ryan*
> *on the telephone. And even if someone messed up, they*
> *went right on with it. How bad we sounded when we sang!*
> *Hearing Tina cry for her sister. Feeling like I was about*
> *to cry every time during that scene and the end of the last*
> *scene. NOT feeling like puking from nervousness for the*
> *last two shows. And, OMG, we did it!*

> *Seeing our family grow close to each other and really start*
> *connecting. Feeling strong, and sad, and pissed off, and*
> *confident. And I could really feel Maxwell coming out of me.*

> *When Syrene gave the lighted candle to Mary M, and Mary's*
> *hair was lit up by the candlelight. When Syrene talked about*
> *Dancers for Peace, then gave Kestrel a hug. When Isis and*
> *Magpie danced together. When we started singing 'Where*
> *Have All the Flowers Gone.' When A- as Syrene said, 'Even*
> *old people.' When I said, 'Can I be in it?' and she hugged me.*
> *Holding the sign in the demo. And freezing at the end, when*
> *the soldier came out.*

Standing up out of the wheel chair in the last scene.

Bring able to actually go out and be my character. The magic. The energy. The feeling of success.

When Kestrel and Caroline danced on the very top of the table. Saying that line, 'We filled them with Pepsi' and then seeing the look on Magpie's face. When Syrene said, 'No— I hope not. We saw a lot of wasted people in Berkeley.'

The anticipation of doing the pre-play, and then the show. How relaxed the actors were onstage. How thrilled the audience was.

The play. The cards, the dark, the light, the there, the gone. The candles. The blood.

When I started acting I felt I was that person and not myself, even if I saw someone I knew in the audience. It was a pretty cool thing to feel. Whoever I was playing, I felt I was adding life to the scene I was in. I was the icing on the cake.

When I played John-John, I really felt like him. I actually felt annoyed when Magpie wouldn't let me go to the light show. It made me feel like Magpie worried about us too much and wouldn't let us do anything. Dennis and Max were really important because Max thinks we should stop the war by force, and Dennis thinks we should stop it with peace. And it was important when Dennis said, 'Blood will have blood.' [from *Macbeth*]

I could see Mary's wings as I said her lines. They were beautiful, white and gray. I could see the singe marks, and feel the scars.

183

As Maxwell unfolded, I felt the feelings and the stress, the relationships between everyone. I realized how they are all connected.

I was able to experience the magic in a way I never have before. It enhanced my ability as an actor. And the play gave me a new perspective on history.

The best thing about it was the memories, totally the memories. Without experiences like this, a lot of friendships wouldn't have happened, and there would be a lot of hate. Nothing would be the same.

Tina reading Marty's letter. And Curbstone reading the letter at the end, so sad.

I- as Denizen, in the scene with Maxwell: very cool. And the stage set-up for Rivendell, so many levels, also very cool. S- crying as Tina—I wanted to look at her so badly, but I was frozen [as Marty] and couldn't.

Tina Blue, 'It's this fricking war!" Feeling sad when Marty is MIA, and mad when Maxwell is yelling at Dennis.

Hearing the audience crying, gasping, laughing. And the actors, too. Feeling like I wanted to run away and hide.

I think I got to the point where I really was Caroline, and it was a blast. I was like, I can't do it, but then I did it, and I am so happy. But I felt bad when her mom died and she didn't know, that was sad.

The more times I was Marty, the more times I was able to cry onstage and feel her pain. Marty had a big part to play in Tina's life.

*I hope the audience understood how powerful this play is,
and how stupidly people can act sometimes.*

*It was really fun and interesting to do, because it's happy
and sad at the same time. And it's also kinda different
from a lot of stuff, and takes place in a different time, too,
which made it harder. And it matters because all the people
who believe in Peace will see it and understand it.*

The Vietnam War was a whirlpool that moved through the lives of
everyone in the United States, and all the people in *Bring the War Home*
get caught up in its vortex. Even when people believe they are on the
same side, war has a way of destroying the sibling, family, and community bonds that usually keep us together. In this play, the struggles to do
the right thing, to be loyal, to find out who you are, to correct injustice,
and to heal the hearts and bodies of others are all affected by what was
happening 8,000 miles away. As we have discovered so many times over
the past 50 years, the scars left by those struggles last forever.

But with every struggle comes some chance for redemption, for
making meaning out of the suffering. Tina Blumenthal, Syrene Lawrence,
Dennis Swantner, others in this play, and thousands of people in the real-
life peace movement found that meaning in reaching out to each other,
in re-establishing the connections that are the basis of our humanity.

In the same way, the struggle to tell the difficult story of *Bring the
War Home* helped my students deal with the issues it raises, and with
the conflicts in their own lives. Everyone wants a happy ending; and the
ending of the play is hopeful in one sense, because it shows people reaching out to each other, forming stronger, life-affirming connections. The
unavoidable tragedy of all war is, by necessity, also there. As with *Hamlet*,
however, the actors felt that the success of their presentation was another
kind of answer to conflict.

Horatio, Hamlet, and Marcellus. [*Hamlet*]

Better Than I Could Devise

After Changeling's final performance of *Winter's Tale* in 2008, I suggested to the departing actors that it would be great to get together in a few years and do one more play. "When I retire," I told them, "you can all come back and we'll do one last *Hamlet*." This was a pipe dream and I knew it. Soon, they would all be going off to college, or finding jobs in Seattle. But it was a nice pipe dream. We all knew that going out with a bang meant doing *Hamlet,* and even though it had only been a year since the last version, several of us had already talked about new ways of doing it. Every year there was a new film version, or a new Royal Shakespeare Company production that had been extensively reviewed, and new staging ideas were constantly circulating.

Then, in 2010, the Oregon Shakespeare Festival put the play on again—but this time, the lead role was played by Dan Donohue, a long-time favorite of all the older kids. Through the years, we had seen him play many famous roles brilliantly: Mercutio, Caliban, Simon Stimson, Sir Andrew Aguecheek [*Twelfth Night*], Puck, and Touch-stone were the ones we remembered best. As usual, a large group of us descended on Ashland that summer, for 4 days of frisbee, fudge, Italian food, and Shakespeare. *Hamlet* was amazing, and we saw quite a few things we could steal borrow. If, that is, we ever did the play again....

As I began my last school year, I began to hear rumors about semi-secret plans to do *Hamlet* the following summer. By this time the ex-Changelings were scattered all over the place, however, and I figured it was just wishful thinking. Finally, in the fall, my curiosity got the best of me. I emailed the two people I pegged as the co-conspirators. I said look, what you're thinking about is impossible. You'll all be working, or returning to college, or (in a couple of cases) graduating from college and looking for work. It's a nice gesture, thank you ever so much, but it's crazy. The response was quick and characteristically blunt: *"Shut up! We already have the time blocked out, 15 people are in for sure, and we'll get the rest. It's happening!"*

The young woman who had been my first assistant director, and who now had an acting degree, took charge of script-cutting and casting, and let me know that we would be "co-directors." The young woman who had played Hamlet in 2007, now in her final year of college in Boston, proclaimed herself the producer and publicist and artistic director—and oh yes, she was playing Hamlet again, only with a bigger script. A few months later, I got the new script—about 20 pages longer than the last one we used—with orders to figure out and incorporate ALL the blocking by April.

Miraculously, and mostly by long distance at first, the production began to come together. Several of the wonderful parent-angels who had supported our theater program for years signed on—notably, Patsy for the costumes, and Paul for the lights. The producer launched a Kickstarter site and raised some money, then she created a beautiful poster to put up around the area. The director sent out email after email to the cast, not only the completed script (with blocking), but also contact lists, costume recommendations, and rehearsal schedules. Finding a rehearsal location turned out to be almost impossible, but finally one of the cast families let us use their barn and tarp-shaded yard. At the very last minute, a recently-restored theater was engaged—for a sum that made my jaw drop, but the producer insisted we could do it. Shows were scheduled for the second week in August.

By the middle of July, people began drifting into town, and we got under way. The same kids who in 2007 had played Claudius, Laertes, Ophelia, the Ghost, the Gravedigger, and Osric were back. My co-director was playing Gertrude. Several cast members were forced to drop out, but replacements were found. Rehearsals began. The impossible seemed possible, even though the Player Queen was going to summer school 80 miles away, and couldn't make most practices; and Laertes was working in Seattle and could only get away occasionally late at night; and Polonius was doing a research project in Olympia and couldn't make any except the last few rehearsals. Three days before the first show, we moved into the actual theater, set up shop, and desperately tried to have complete run-throughs, usually with two to five cast members missing. It was a typical Changeling production, but with one huge difference: everyone knew it was going to be okay.

How did they know? Because they had known each other, and worked together, for so many years. Watching the rehearsals, I saw lots of new moves, new ideas, new parts of the script that had been added. The closer we got to the first performance, the more risks the actors took, as they fell back into the comfort zone of working with friends—in some cases, with people they had known since pre-school. I was impressed, and excited for the opening. And as I watched, I couldn't keep from remembering. Every actor's speech and gestures and movements—even refined as they were by years of experience—sent me tripping back into the past.

I saw Horatio, now a tall, muscular college student, and remembered him being Laertes ten years before, holding his sword to the throat of his best friend, who was playing Claudius. When we rehearsed the Mousetrap scene, the young man who was playing the Gravedigger was doubling as the Players' fiddler. Watching the easy way he had with his violin, I thought of how I had pushed him into doing Lysander, back when he was shy; of his breakthrough performance as Macduff; and of all the times I had seen him busking on the street in Ashland, raking in more spending money than the other kids had ever seen. Playing Polonius was D-, now doing research in microbiology; but to me he would always be Touchstone in a goofy golf hat, and a perfect Prospero in *The Tempest*, way back at the very beginning.

The actor playing Claudius was putting the finishing touches on our custom-made stage piece, a rectangular platform that would enable us to do most of the show in the round. I remembered him best as Bottom, but he had performed so many other memorable roles: Oberon, Camillo in *Winter's Tale*, Demetrius, the Ghost, Snug the Joiner, Theseus, Macduff, Claudio in *Much Ado*, and many others. Now he was playing in regional theater, and we were lucky to have him with us. Helping him out with the carpentry was a close friend, playing Gildenstern for us. The two of them had made one movie already, another was in the works. The friend had also been with us for years. He had played Horatio, Cleomenes and the Shepherd in *Winter's Tale,* a wonderfully innocent Osric in the 2007 *Hamlet,* Egeus, four different roles in Macbeth, and many other parts. Among our group, he was most famous for wearing the bear suit in *Winter's Tale,* terrorizing poor Antigones, and remarking in the survey, *"Being the bear is taking a serious toll on my social life."*

Hanging out together, as they had been for the last five or six years, were the two ninth-graders for whom this was the first *Hamlet,* but whose talents and experience made them essential to any Changeling production. SZ was the Player King, who had been given a much bigger role than ever before, and Marcellus. Master memorizer and able to play any kind of role that was needed, having her there was like having an all-star utility infielder who also just happens to be able to catch and, oh yes, has a 92-miles-per-hour fastball. Every time I needed someone to back up a role, or take over a lead when someone got sick or dropped out, she was there and had it memorized in one or two days. Her Mrs. Gibbs, in *Our Town,* was the role I remembered best, but Mercutio was a close second, and I'll never forget her red bandana and pitch-perfect dry wit as the Wobbly radical in *Hard Times.* Her friend SM, the one who would "never, ever, ever, ever" forget being Emily in *Our Town,* had a long history of what she called "dragon-slaying," i.e., conquering her shyness by pushing herself and succeeding at being assertive people onstage: Beatrice, Rosalind, and Miranda (*Hard Times*) were the stepping stones to finding her voice. If you asked her, however, she'd probably say she had more fun playing Verges (Dogberry's sidekick), or the simple rustic William in *As You Like It,* or doing the bunny hop as a Watchman in *Much Ado.* In *Hamlet,* she was playing Rosencranz and Bernardo.

The Ghost of Hamlet's father was a young man with the best voice of any actor I ever had—not quite in the bass range, but strong and low; combined with his excellent articulation, it made him perfect for this role—which he had also played in 2007. He loved reciting the Ghost's extended catalog of Claudius's abuses to Hamlet, the discovery speech, where Hamlet's father reveals his murder to his son; and I loved hearing him say it, with just the right inflections and pauses, and just enough emotion, in all the right places. We had always cut this long passage somewhat, but R- kept adding to it, and for this version, where the length of the play was not an issue, he had put in the lines he had always wanted to say:

> *But virtue, as it never will be moved,*
> *Though lewdness court it in a shape of heaven,*
> *So lust, though to a radiant angel linked,*
> *Will sate itself in a celestial bed,*
> *And prey on garbage.*

The word "garbage" cuts the line short, and both syllables are stressed, most likely indicating that it should get extra emphasis, followed by a pause. Our Hamlet was kneeling in shock and fear as these words were being said, and with this line, R- leaned down and slowly poured the word "garbage" directly into Hamlet's ear—just as Claudius had done with the poison when he murdered Hamlet's father. It was perfect. I remembered so well watching R- develop as an actor. He had been many of the great authority figures, of course—Theseus, Oberon, Macbeth, and Polixenes. He had also been Lysander, and a sweetly androgynous Flute. But no one would ever forget him as a strikingly made-up and calmly malicious Puck in 2006.

Our Laertes, finally free from work and Seattle music gigs for a week, was practicing swordplay with Hamlet. Coached by my co-director, who learned stage combat as part of her acting degree, they had been rehearsing the duel for days. For the fight to be serious and convincing, it had to be risky enough to be dangerous, hence the long hours of practice. These two had fought onstage four years before, and they were determined to make this duel even better. I admired the young man playing Laertes a great deal, for of all the cast, his struggle had been the hardest. Not to learn how to act—he was pretty much a natural—but to survive when his parents broke up. When he came into my class as a fifth-grader, he wore his backpack all day, he was so uncertain about where he belonged after school. He was constantly shuffled from one parent to another, sometimes even to a grandparent an hour away. In spite of it all, at school he found not one but two safe places of refuge: our program, where he soon made several close friends, and the stage, where he could leave everything behind and just be someone else. Someone like Benedick in *Much Ado*, who knew exactly who he was, and who gave I- his first real taste of self-confidence. Like Oberon, whose magic brought him alive. And most of all, like Laertes: loyal, impetuous, emotionally transparent, and in the end, beautifully forgiving.

On the center platform, our Player Queen was practicing her back bends and cartwheels for the players' prologue. This amazing young woman was, and always had been, our spark, our power source. She was taking summer classes at a college 90 minutes and a long ferry ride away and could get to only a few rehearsals, but she wouldn't have missed this play for anything. M- had also played many standout roles in the past ten years: Margaret and Benedick in *Much Ado*, Maria and Boyet in *Love's Labor's Lost*, even the crazy priest in *As You Like It*. But for her, Puck was the end-all and be-all, and the way she had incorporated acrobatics and her electric charisma into the 2006 *MND* was what always came back to me when she appeared. Like several kids down through the years, she believed that the role of Puck was very close to her core identity:

> *Words cannot express the impact drama has made on*
> *my life. Often I find myself trying to stay open and free,*
> *trying to find the person I was in sixth grade, the true*
> *me. You first introduced me to this person in fifth grade,*
> *when I played Puck for the first time. That wandering*
> *spirit is always inside me, and when I start to lose myself*
> *I always find my way back through Puck.*

Puck's mysterious, shifting identity and dual personality, his ability to be so many of the thousand clowns—and yet still retain his wise and enigmatic aura—was invariably appealing to kids on the verge of adolescence. Yes, we all have to grow up—but not by contracting ourselves into frozen, anxious automatons. We can grow up by expanding ourselves into the lives of others, by throwing ourselves into the multi-dimensional characters who live in the imaginary world of the theater. Of all those worlds, Faery (and especially Puck's central place there) is the one that helped my kids the most. Is this escapism? I love what C.S. Lewis said. When Tolkien asked who would be most hostile to escapist literature, Lewis answered, "The jailers." The cages into which our culture confines adolescents are mostly invisible to them. They don't realize they are trapped until they experience the liberation that music, or art, or theater can bring. Like a good baseball scout, Puck is always on the lookout for talent.

The young woman playing Ophelia is another example of this phenomenon. Watching her rehearse being insane was painful for me, because what I saw behind that mask was a multitude of wildly funny and happy faces: the second-grader who found out who she "really was" by being a fairy in *MND*; the sixth-grader whose bizarrely-lipsticked Thisby almost stopped a performance (because I fell down laughing backstage); the ditzy Hermia who attached herself to Lysander like a leech; the middle-schooler whose virtuoso improvising as Puck saved a show when our lighting system went out; and so many others. It was learning to be all those clowns that gave G- the confidence and security to reach out for bigger roles, and to learn to show other, deeper feelings. And so, she became Margaret (*Much Ado*), Hecate and Lady Macduff in *Macbeth*, Perdita in *Winter's Tale*, and finally, in 2007, Hamlet's mother. For years, she seemed to be everywhere, filling in for missing fairies or Pucks, choreographing every single *MND* dance, and always, helping younger kids learn to take the same leaps and risks she had taken. When we decided that, in her madness, Ophelia would both regress to childhood and lose every inhibition the daughter of a King's adviser could lose, G- showed no fear at all. Her ability to throw herself completely into Ophelia—knowing her old friend S- (playing Horatio) was there to catch her—was no surprise to the cast, but it was shocking to the audience: she wore the bloody shirt of her dead father (stabbed by Hamlet), lunged at the King, and sang Ophelia's eerie songs as though possessed. In contrast to her earlier innocence, the effect was quite powerful.

Some actors believe that Ophelia's last scene with Hamlet, just before the Mousetrap play, is as hard as the madness, because it's so difficult to know what Ophelia is feeling. In the face of his cruel attack, with the King and Queen watching them, how is she supposed to react? Does she still hope they can be reconciled? Is she already showing signs of the despair that later becomes madness? Or is she coldly angry, having given up on their relationship? From her words, it is difficult to know. For the young woman who was playing Hamlet, his manic bitterness in this scene is a weapon. Since the King and Ophelia's father had used Ophelia as a pawn to trap him, Hamlet would counter with a coldly cynical manipulation of his own—turning Ophelia's face and heart to stone. As Hamlet—until he accepts his fate—K- always tried to push things right to the edge. Pretending to be crazy, overreacting to everything, paranoid about the slightest remark, at this point in the play her Hamlet was always keeping score.

K- was the only actor in the cast who had been in every Changeling production of Hamlet. As a sixth-grader, she had been Bernardo and Rosencranz, in awe of the older kids—especially J-, who played Hamlet. Three years later, she was Ophelia to his final Hamlet. In 2007, she finally got her chance to play the lead role—*"Somehow I guess I knew that I was to play Hamlet."* An all-star softball pitcher, K- was extremely competitive. Whether by choice, unconsciously, or simply because of her breezy, outgoing, and assertive personality, her portrait of Hamlet was designed to clash with that of J-. Where J- was deliberate, uncertain by design, thoughtful, and gracefully self-contained onstage, K- was decisive and gracefully active—always right in the King's face, flat on her back to start the "to be" speech, raving at Ophelia, and savagely brutal to Polonius.

Both Hamlets were after the truth. For J-, it was a logic puzzle to be solved. For K-, it was a prey animal to be hunted down. Since the role is a paradigm of ambiguity, both approaches were legitimate and effective. Here is one thing I remember: at the end of the play, J- (also an athlete) was pale with exhaustion, and K- looked like a hunter holding a trophy. Wearing Hamlet's masks had changed them both.

In this version of the play, Hamlet's rashness was tempered by the fact that G- was a different kind of Ophelia than before. M- (who played Ophelia in 2007) had been personally wounded, emotionally raw, and new to acting; her Ophelia was fragile. This time, Ophelia was much more confident; she seemed strong even in her vulnerability and her madness—more her own person, and better suited to be Hamlet's lover. In performance, it made a huge difference for Hamlet.

Along these lines, the other significant difference for Hamlet this time was how well he was balanced by the performance of the young woman playing Gertrude. Instead of being overpowered, C- was a perfect match for K-. They had been good friends for ten years, and they had been the heart of the conspiracy to put the play together. Both were fearless, exacting, obsessive about acting, and crazy—in a good way, of course.

All Gertrudes walk a tightrope between helplessness and cynicism. We the audience never know for sure how much she knows—or how much she doesn't want to know, or won't admit to herself. In the first half of the play, C-'s Gertrude is an elegant parade queen in high heels and glittery smile, projecting a self-confidence she doesn't quite believe, all the while hanging on to Claudius as if to a life ring. Royally solicitous to her troubled son, it's obvious that she has completely lost touch with him while he has been away, and still treats him like a child. Always pretending things are just dandy, as the play goes on she makes us more and more anxious: does she really believe this act of hers, or is it part of some horrible plan?

When Hamlet confronts her, in the famous "closet scene," the actress is forced to make a choice: she can collapse into self-pity, and lead us to forgive her too soon (because even if she's sorry for herself, we still don't know if it's real); or, she can decide to take seriously the image of Claudius that Hamlet is showing her, and begin to distance herself from him. At this point in our play, Gertrude began to drink—but not, as do some Gertrudes, to escape and forget; C- showed us a woman who drank to give herself courage—both the courage to keep up appearances in court, and the courage to try and live up to Hamlet's harsh verbal challenges.

In these endgame scenes, I watched C- work very deliberately to slow down the story, to brake Hamlet's rush to self-destruction—and in so doing, to build the dramatic tension to an even higher pitch. It's the end of the closet scene; Hamlet has just murdered Polonius (hiding behind the arras) in her bedroom, and C- shows the shock in her whole being as Hamlet *"lugs the guts"* away. C- takes an extended pause here: head in hands, she is half in tears, half angry at fate—we finally get to see what remains after the parade queen mask falls off. As the lights fade, she mutters an almost guttural curse and slams the wine bottle down on her table—a glimpse into her psyche, but still not the answer to all of our questions. What if it's just another act?

When Laertes appears, demanding to know why Polonius's murder was covered up, Gertrude still protects her husband. But Ophelia's madness and death are too much for her; at the end of the scene, despite Claudius's plea, she turns her back on him and walks away.

Because of the way C- has played her, in the last scene we are able to accept Gertrude's death not as the result of a character flaw, not just as Claudius's evil turning on itself, and not just as an accident, but as a sacrifice. Daring to directly challenge her husband—he tells her not to drink the wine that was intended for Hamlet, but she says, *"I will, my lord,"* she is finally standing up to him; and then C- adds the rest sarcastically, *"I pray you, pardon me."* As she dies, she tells *"my dear Hamlet"* that she was poisoned, and Hamlet's brutal vengeance on the King becomes an act not just on his father's behalf, but also on hers. By keeping alive in Hamlet and in the audience the possibility that Gertrude is redeemable, even in her weakness and possible complicity, C- has walked the tightrope brilliantly.

All this, from that little fifth-grader who leaped onto the stage as Laertes so long ago; that Puck-obsessed sixth-grader, removing her make-up as she spoke the epilogue; that seventh-grade Ophelia, who first showed us how to find your self by losing it. Now, as opening night for our last-ever Hamlet approached, she was using her acting-school training to put it all together. She made a sweetly formal show of asking my opinion about blocking issues that came up during these last rehearsals, but I knew, and she knew, that she already had the answers: she had been thinking about doing this play her way for at least five years. For the first time, I was able to do what real directors do at this point: fade into the woodwork and watch. And remember.

Thursday night came, opening night, but without any obvious anxiety. Excited at being reunited, the cast had been doing some late-night get-togethers, even when we were in final rehearsals, and the parties only seemed to make the play better. In a sense, this play was what we had been pointing toward—without knowing it—for 12 years. It was the culmination of a lot of trust-building, a lot of character-building, and a lot of cast circles on that tiny little stage in my classroom. But instead of being a final exam, it turned out to be a celebration. It celebrated all that we had learned—about Hamlet, about working together as a family, and about ourselves, as actors and as people. And it put our final stamp on this most famous play in the English language.

That sounds delusional, I know. I don't mean that our version was better than any other, that *would* be delusional. But after watching my actors for so many years, what I saw in the performances helped me recognize that we had definitely evolved a way of staging Shakespeare—any play—that was uniquely ours.

One thing I always noticed was that they were constantly searching for useful symbols and images and gestures of connection and disconnection. For them, Hamlet was about isolation—how it happens, what it looks like, and how isolated people try to re-connect with others and themselves. Onstage, this was embodied in their many (often unconscious) movements and gestures of reaching out, turning away, pushing away, embracing, holding onto, shielding, and comforting. While she still believed in him, Gertrude was always either arm-in-arm with Claudius or holding his arm with both hands, and as they sat watching the Mousetrap, they were very loving to each other, kissing occasionally, and holding hands. When she abandons him, it is not with words, but by turning her back and walking away.

The first time we see Hamlet and Ophelia together, just before the "coronation scene," they secretly kiss, then she runs over to stand by her father. A simple gesture, but it solidly establishes their relationship, even before a line is spoken. In the chapel scene, Hamlet is violent, almost physically abusive in his contact with her.

When Laertes and Ophelia say goodbye to each other, it is with a hug; then, she takes off her scarf and places it around his neck. Again, the simple protective gesture of a caring sister. At her funeral, Laertes lingers to take one last look at her in the grave. Just before the grave is closed, very spontaneously, he takes off the scarf and drops it in. Putting his hand on Laertes' shoulder, the attending priest—who has just refused Ophelia the normal rites of burial, because she may have committed suicide—tries to atone by offering a bit of physical support. Laertes will have none of it, and slaps away the priest's hand.

The wandering players who stop at Elsinore, and get caught up in Hamlet's Mousetrap, seem to be the only simple and true friends he has in the whole play: he speaks to them as to brothers and sisters, for they are actors just as he is, and therefore wise to the hidden meanings behind masks. After the Player King has "auditioned" Priam's speech, Hamlet bids them a temporary goodbye; this actor turns to leave, then turns back, takes off her scarf, and puts it around Hamlet's neck.

When Ophelia takes physical leave of her senses before the King and Queen, throws herself at him and becomes violent, it is the stoic Horatio who intervenes, by tenderly holding her arms from behind as she rages and weeps and screams.

And at the very end, when Hamlet dies, it is not isolated and alone; finally allowing himself to touch his dearest friend, Horatio kneels and embraces Hamlet in his final agony. *None of these gestures were directed in the script.* But for our actors— again, usually unconsciously—they were a huge part of the story. This is what it *feels* like to be accepted, or rejected, or to indicate or accept solidarity and love, or even—in the case of Gertrude and Claudius— to pretend these feelings. As happened so many times over the years, my actors understood and presented the play as a story of relationships. Hamlet was not simply a man forced into speaking *"wild and whirling words"* because of what happened to his father; another part of it was that he had no one to turn to. Forbidden Ophelia's presence by Polonius, and unable or unwilling to confide in Horatio, suspicious of his mother, the social context forces him into isolation. He pretends an off-and-on madness, but not to the players, with whom he is his natural, outgoing self. The irony that he can only be real in the company of professional pretenders highlights how dysfunctional his social environment really is.

The other wonderful irony of the players' appearance, as Hamlet notices, is that in their acting they are able to express their feelings honestly and directly—the Player King weeps as he tells Priam's story. That is, they can do what Hamlet knows he cannot, grieve openly. He internalizes this as a character flaw, but in the ice palace created by Claudius, Polonius, and even Gertrude, it's clearly impossible. Our actors' consistent use of connecting gestures and tableaux were very effective in showing this.

Within our program, within my classroom, and within the smaller family of Changeling, the integrity of the social fabric was the foundation for all effective work and learning. To the degree that we could create true interdependence, to that degree was success possible—both individual success, and the success of such group efforts as the production of a

Shakespeare play. *"Everyone does better when everyone does better"*—such a tired cliche; but, like Shakespeare's words, it actually did *"sink into our souls."*

The five performances of Hamlet went very smoothly, and were well-received. We told a bigger version of the story than ever before, and we told it in a way that reflected both the history of our theater project and the core values of our program. As a play, it was a scourge to many of our dearest illusions, and also a powerful tribute to our courage in facing the truth, as I believe it was meant to be. As a retirement gift, it was by far the best I could ever have imagined.

photo by Isabel Gates

Hamlet and Laertes. [*Hamlet*]

photo by Isabel Gates

Oberon and Titania. [*A Midsummer Night's Dream*]

That Which Knitteth Souls
and Prospers Loves

Probably the best-known of all optical illusions is that famous picture of the wine goblet which, if seen in a different way, becomes two facing profiles. Supposedly, seeing both images simultaneously is impossible, although some of my students invariably insisted they could do it, and perhaps they could. What always fascinated me was the prospect that maybe, if you really concentrated, you could actually see one image change into the other.

When I looked at my student actors onstage and saw, at the same time, their younger selves, I almost believed it was possible to see both images—this young person both being and becoming.

When we look at progressive pictures of kids in a family album, what we notice—almost always—is what is different. And usually, the most recent picture subtly and quickly shifts the image in our brain, so that now we have a new idea of that person. "Look how you've changed," we say, meaning, "Look how my idea of you has changed." But the young person at whose image we are gazing still contains her younger self, and in some ways always will. As adults, we want to see—and therefore do see—the emerging adult. But consider what we miss: the transformation itself; the two-images-in-one.

I submit—joined by Shakespeare, as I hope to show—that the recent picture, and even the older ones, are masks. Not by design, but by the very nature of things.

If we know the actors personally, transformations are obvious. We see both, the daughter/son/student, and the character in the play. If we're perceptive, and lucky, sometimes we get to see both at once. Part of us wants so badly to take the most recent image for "the truth"—look, she's all grown up. Another part of us refuses to believe in the change, and is relieved when the costume is off and the "real person" appears from backstage when the last act is over—he's growing up too fast. This is where Shakespeare comes in. It's all real, he says in so many places—and also, none of it is real. And the transformations are fascinating, and make great subjects for stories. All those faces are masks, for we are all actors, constantly adapting the image we show to the world—masking it, making it up (with make-up or without), faking it, unmasking it, hiding or revealing ourselves in ways we don't even admit. We learn who we are by pretending, by trying out different roles. All of us, and especially adolescents, are constantly changing and being changed, and our natural response is to pretend—"pre - tend," originally meaning to "stretch out" or "to extend." By pretending, we are extending ourselves, expanding our personalities and reaching out to others in empathy. Actors are by definition people who are stretching themselves, trying to find out which costumes and faces will fit and be useful. It's so interesting that the same verb, "to act," means both "to pretend" and "to do something decisively." Even the word itself is an act, an etymological one-man show, playing several parts with only three letters.

Hamlet is Shakespeare's pre-eminent example. He plays many roles in Shakespeare's tale—indeed, he is constantly acting. At the beginning of the play, Hamlet talks disparagingly about *"actions that a man might play,"* as opposed to *"that which passeth show."* Starting almost immediately after that line, Hamlet becomes an actor. He is at least four different people just to Ophelia—a tender lover, a manic tyrant, a fool, and a guilt-ridden avenger. As his mother watches, he turns from dutiful son to Grand Inquisitor to guilt-free murderer. With the players, he transforms himself into an actual director, dictating to them the basic principles of good acting—then reverts to being their noble friend. He puts on the *"manic disposition"* for Polonius and Claudius, and takes it off for Rosencranz and Gildenstern—to then become first their frat-boy pal, then their lie-detector, then their righteous torturer.

Just before the end, he seems finally to decide who he really is: someone who will accept his fate, and take what comes. In a final irony, however, when the duel happens he is forced into another role, that of heroic avenger.

He has created his character from nothing, like a playwright…
he is the author and architect of his own being…he constructs
many characters for himself in the course of the play, ending
as the avenging hero he initially found it so difficult to enact.
He can act only when he is acting.
—Colin McGinn, *Shakespeare's Philosophy*

Even at the end, we are still left with the mystery of who Hamlet
"really" is. But for Shakespeare, it is the mystery itself, the multiplicity of
Hamlet's selves, that is the reality. And it is through watching his transformations into these various selves that we discover the most about him,
about the play, and about ourselves.

Puck is another example, and *A Midsummer Night's Dream* is the
textbook of transformation. After Puck transforms Bottom, Quince
panics: *"Bless thee, Bottom, thou art—translated!"* One of the oldest
translations of "translated" is "removed to another sphere," which is
what happens to Bottom. And to the other mortals in the play: workers
are translated into actors; lovers are turned into haters, then back into
lovers; friends are turned into enemies, then back into friends—but
different; Flute is turned into a woman, just as the actors themselves
change gender.

By removing something to another sphere, sometimes we make
it easier to see, and understand. Theater isolates emotions in charged,
enchanted situations, so that we might use the energy as a catalyst, for
transformations. Think of acid tests, and crucibles, and cloud chambers.
And alchemy, of course.

Actors too, if they allow it to happen, may also be blessed by
translation—may also be changed, their ordinary lives transcended by
that which transpires onstage. "Trans" meaning "across"—to go across a
divide, to step (or be pulled) across a line, or onto a stage. To be born, to
die. To sleep, perchance to be transformed.

> *Drama has played an extremely big role in my life. It
> made me a different person, and made me realize that
> life is just a big role. Everybody has one, and they're
> all important to our play. Whatever your actions do,
> they are the improv of your life.*

It was a very good experience for me. When I played my character, I could really let go of who I am, and become who I need to be.

Drama has meant a lot to me this year. When my grandma died I tried to hide from myself when we were rehearsing. I pretended I did not know myself.

One of the most important things I learned and won't forget is that I have more power than I thought. Not just physically but verbally, the power of cleverness and sad- ness and…. forgiveness, even when I haven't done anything. I learned how things work. This will be hard to explain, but no matter how young you are, you can be who you want to be, and then you can know.

Drama helped me open my heart out into the world.

I was really mad and sad about what was happening at home, but here I can be someone else, and forget that other stuff.

My life is far from good right now, and I like being the best I can in someone else's life.

I remember the glare of the lights. Hearing the concern and love in kids' voices. The fear that runs through your body. The smell of sweat from hard acting, throwing ourselves into it. The feeling of love and trust, knowing that when you fall, somebody will catch you.

I remember the audience's faces and the sounds of their gasps. And the quiet backstage. And the feeling that we were actually doing it, and that it finally came to life.

I really felt good. I can connect with Michael because, in the beginning of the play, Michael's not at all happy, but it gets better and better and better. At the beginning of the year I hated myself. But it's getting better.

*I remember the sights of hard work and people caring
for one another. The sounds of lines of wisdom being
said, and the emotions of love, hate, and friendship. The
feelings of connection or of fear, before a fight scene or
an important line.*

*I remember feeling so nervous I thought I wouldn't be
able to do it. But then I stepped onstage and SHE took
over. I remember saying my last line of the last performance, I felt relieved and utterly upset at the same time.*

*It helped me let go and relax and let my character decide
what happens next. "Drama helps you see the world
more clearly."*

*"Look, I can't tell you everything, but the world's full of
amazing things." In life there are some bad things, like
Skellig stuck in the garage, but once you move out of
those you might see something amazing—like wings!*

*After the last Hamlet, I tried in vain to sort things out in
a way that conveys what all of it meant to me. It's tough!
I do re-live that part of my life every day, though. Doing
Shakespeare at age 11, dissecting the complexities of the
language, and leaping outside of my comfort zone before
I'd even hit puberty have had more of an impact on my
adult life than any other childhood event. I'm empathetic.
I'm not apologetic for my whackiness. And I'm eternally
grateful to my fellow actors. I'm so proud of that experience.*

*Before I came here, I was very, very shy. But once I came
into this class, I started to talk more, and to speak up for
myself. Drama helped me a lot with my shyness, and to
know who I really am inside.*

*I will never forget that class. The humor, the niceness, the
way kids could be who they wanted to be, and not like stuck-up*

*robots. The plays helped us to be ourselves. When I first came
into that class, being in a play helped me open a secret door
that I was curious about for years, and finally it was open.
I had opened a door totally opposite from "Pandora's Box."
This door was full of hope, confidence, and happiness. Whenever I stepped onstage, I was a totally new person. I was Hero,
Snout, or Philostrate. I have met those people and learned
from them, and I met other people on the way.*

*I was falling apart, but I feel a lot more together now, thanks
to doing theater. You will never know how much this has
helped, including all the Shakespeare. It has saved my life.
I feel like a restored person. I benefitted immensely from it,
and I learned so much!*

The students in my class, wearing masks, transporting themselves
onto a small platform sixteen inches high, en - couraged themselves to
be transformed. And so the audience, suspending their disbelief, may
also be carried across a line, translated into some recognition of what we
share. Spellbound, possibly. Surrendering to the Inner Puck—that's the
key.

Just who *is* Puck? The very first thing we find out about him is his
dual identity—he is both "Hobgoblin" (the imp, the mischief maker)
and also "Robin Goodfellow" (who *"brings good luck"*). He is the chief
transformer—turning Bottom into donkey, lovers into fools—but he is
also the actor with the most roles, i.e. the one who transforms himself the
most. He pretends to be a stool, a crabapple, a lion, a bear, other animals,
Lysander, Demetrius, and finally, a...mortal human? An actor?

*If we shadows have offended,
Think but this, and all is mended:
That you have but slumbered here
While these visions did appear,
And this weak and idle theme,
No more yielding but a dream.
Gentles, do not reprehend:
if you pardon, we will mend:*

And, as I am an honest Puck,
If we have unearned luck
Now to 'scape the serpent's tongue,
We will make amends ere long;
Else the Puck a liar call;
So, good night unto you all.
Give me your hands, if we be friends,
And Robin shall restore amends.

"Shadows" were actors, possibly from the kind of puppet show using shadows. The shadow self is one of our many roles, and not one to be taken lightly...Puck tries to explain it all as a dream: but who is explaining this to us? A fairy? An actor? Both? If you slowly remove your make-up (what makes you up) as you say these lines, you blur the line between the selves; between the worlds. You part the curtain, and let us see the transformation itself.

Puck was one of the biggest chances I've ever
taken. I actually wouldn't call it a chance, it was more
of a jump, a jump onto the stage, into the new me. A
new me in both ways, character and person. As I worked
on the stage more, I changed more. As Puck I learned
so much, not things that you would expect, not acting
but feeling. Feeling everything and sucking in every
drop. I learned the stories of life, like Aesop's Fables,
where there's a moral that goes along with it. I learned
so much about other people, and about myself, too.
It was as though the whole world flew by, and every-
thing you could know and do, you could learn here.
Everything about you and them. The whole world was
laid right in front of you, and you saw it, and in a way
showed the audiences their faults, triumphs, lessons,
life, and you showed them how to accept it. I learned
more onstage than most will ever learn in life. I never
could explain how. You just know it, it's in your bones,
your brain, your soul, your life.

Shakespeare is about the words, saying them
and not knowing what they mean, but at the same time
knowing EXACTLY what they mean. Even when you're
a kid, twelve years old and not even a good reader. It's
about being a kid. Living in a story with fairies and fools
and hoping you'll never wake up but at the same time
knowing you'll have to. It's about going back to the dream
and wishing you could stay there forever. But then looking
around and knowing, you could never go fully back. Then
you know and you wish, you wish with all your heart.
Because you know you would give it all away, just to be
there again. To be twelve and not really knowing what the
world holds for you. Not truly understanding all the bad
things in life, just sensing them. Not caring about what
you were eating for dinner or if your parents would fight
or if your sister would hit you or grades or people or LIFE.
It's about when the lights go down and you walk out on
the stage and the mist surrounds you and you're lost again.
It's like a game, a video game, just hit replay and start
again, start again, start ALL OVER........ again. It's about
when the curtains come down and light through the window
shines in your face again. You look out the window and see
the world—and you want that curtain up again. It's about
protection and love and knowing it's the last performance.
It's about chains being broken. It's about blood being spilt.
It's about your fears and joys and everything you think and
feel coming out of you, and it being okay.

When they wrote about their experiences onstage, my students were fond of using the word "magic." It was a cop-out, of course, a kind of lazy shorthand expression for the complicated process they had just been through. But perhaps not entirely. We think we know all the secrets, but Shakespeare would have laughed. How *do* you explain the way those two wine goblet images change back and forth? Well, the brain does this… and then…ah. At the end of *As You Like It*, Rosalind comes out to give an epilogue. *"My way is to conjure you,"* she says. From the Latin word *conju-*

rare, meaning "to conspire." Theater bands us together, as co-conspirators of the imagination; the lights go down, and we all agree, at least for a time, to believe in magic.

At the end of *The Tempest,* in what is widely held to be Shakespeare's *au revoir* to the stage, Prospero the magician comes out and gives the epilogue, which begins with these lines:

> *Now my charms are all o'erthrown,*
> *And what strength I have's mine own,*
> *Which is most faint.*

The magic is gone, but the spell itself has done its work. Caliban and Ariel, the spirit and the flesh, have been set free; and we the audience—witnesses to their transformations—have been renewed: empowered, enlightened, enchanted. Like Hermia's solemn promise to Lysander in *MND,* we are filled with *"that which knitteth souls and prospers loves."*

From my journal, spring of 2001:

> *We are backstage, just before the first performance*
> *of Hamlet. We are sitting in a circle, sharing our last*
> *thoughts and encouragements. The students' eyes are*
> *shining with excitement and anticipation. There are*
> *no doubts whatsoever. It is like a feeling of water,*
> *before trapped, now about to spill freely over a dam.*
> *The drums start. The play begins. The characters,*
> *and the actors, come totally alive.*

photo by Isabel Gates

Another side of Puck. [*A Midsummer Night's Dream*]

Acknowledgments

Our theater project would never have been sustainable without the loyal support of countless wonderful North Kitsap Options parents down through the years. The fear of omitting someone would prevent a wiser person from singling out a few people, but I feel strongly obligated to say a special thanks to the following, who were there for us year after year, in so many helpful ways: to Ron LeMay, Joe and Penny Beaulieu, Cornelia Gifford, Isabel Gates, Carolina Veenstra, Nada Healy, to Shawn and Paul Larson, to all the parents who did so much, my profound gratitude.

In a category all by themselves are Paul and Patsy Bryan, my necessary angels. Especially at the beginning, you were Prospero and Ariel to my Caliban. You taught me the language to make it work. I'll never forget Paul's supreme confidence—after he took apart the classroom ceiling to install stage lighting, and we were busted by the fire department, the way he always said, "Everything we did is temporary!" Together, you made it so easy to be a fanatic. Thank you.

Thanks to Libby Palmer, for jump-starting my teaching career way back when, and to Sue Dazey, for years of guidance and inspiration.

As for the actors, what can I say about what we did that you haven't already said in these pages? You didn't hide, and many of you discovered what you were trying to hide from. You learned—very well—how to put on the mask, and when to take it off. When one of you fell, someone always caught you. "Love and togetherness"—you weren't afraid to say it. Best of all, you learned who you really are. And because you did it all so beautifully, you changed my life. *"Beggar that I am, I am even poor in thanks, but I thank you."*

As for this book, I want to acknowledge the continued support and encouragement of Eric, Andrew, Christopher, and Suzanne DeWeese. They knew just what to say, and when to say it; and I continue to be inspired by their kindness and integrity.

Thank you to Gwen Moore and Pat Britt at Turtle Press, for taking in a foundling, and to Ruth Marcus, for giving it such a fitting wardrobe—*What shalt thou exchange for rags? Robes.*

And to Kris DeWeese, who made all of it possible, lifelong thanks.

photo by Isabel Gates

Minstrel, Perdita, and Florizel. [*The Winter's Tale*]

About the Author

Robert DeWeese taught grades four through eight in the Options Program of the North Kitsap (Washington State) School District for many years. A lifelong interest in the works of William Shakespeare, and a passion for helping students learn interdependence and mutual trust, led him to build his curriculum around in-class and after-school performances of Shakespeare's plays. Field trips to live theater at Seattle Shakespeare and the Oregon Shakespeare Festival were a regular part of his theater project, and his students performed in parks, nursing homes, shopping malls, and even on board a Washington State ferry, as well as onstage in schools and classrooms. In 2002, the author was one of two Washington State teachers to receive an ING Unsung Heroes Award, honoring his Shakespeare project.

Mr. DeWeese has been involved in alternative education since the early 1980s. Prior to his tenure in Options, he served on the Steering Committee of the Port Townsend (Washington) School District's OPEPO Program for 12 years.

With his family, he owned and operated Melville and Company Books in Port Townsend for 26 years. He holds an M.A. and A.B.D. in American Studies from the University of Texas at Austin.

He is the author of two full-length plays for secondary students. *Hard Times* is centered around the struggle of ordinary families to survive the Great Depression of the 1930s; and *Bring the War Home* is about the conflicts within the movement to resist the war in Vietnam. Both plays are free to interested teachers. To learn more, about these plays or about getting started with Shakespeare in the classroom, contact him at bobbinsdream@gmail.com.

Made in the USA
San Bernardino, CA
23 April 2015